CHOOSING
— *to* —
LEARN
from LIFE

The Circle

CHOOSING
— to —
LEARN
from LIFE

MIKE BREEN
with MAL CALLADINE

Building the New Generation of Believers

COOK COMMUNICATIONS MINISTRIES
Colorado Springs, Colorado • Paris, Ontario
KINGSWAY COMMUNICATIONS LTD
Eastbourne, England

NexGen® is an imprint of
Cook Communications Ministries, Colorado Springs, CO 80918
Cook Communications, Paris, Ontario
Kingsway Communications, Eastbourne, England

CHOOSING TO LEARN FROM LIFE

First printing, 2006
Printed in the United States of America

1 2 3 4 5 6 7 8 9 10 Printing/Year 11 10 09 08 07 06

Cover Design: BrandNavigation, LLC
Cover Photo: PhotoDisc

Mike Breen is the creator and developer of the *LifeShapes* material (formerly called
LifeSkills) and the eight shapes as a memorable method of discipleship.

All Scripture quotations, unless otherwise noted, are taken from the HOLY BIBLE,
NEW INTERNATIONAL VERSION®. Copyright © 1973, 1978, 1984 International
Bible Society. Used by permission of Zondervan. All rights reserved. Scripture quo-
tations marked KJV are from the King James Version of the Bible. (Public Domain.)
Italics added for emphasis.

Library of Congress Cataloging-in-Publication Data

Breen, Mike, Revd.
  Choosing to learn from life / by Mike Breen.-- 1st ed.
    p. cm. -- (Lifeshapes)
  Includes bibliographical references.
  ISBN 0-7814-4296-6
  1. Christian life. I. Title.
  BV4501.3.B744 2006
  248.4--dc22
                        2005024057

This book is dedicated to my daughter Beccy Breen—you are an amazing person and example to us all of how to follow Jesus and learn from him.

Contents

Acknowledgments

J would like to thank Mal Calladine for all of his help and contributions in writing this book. I also want to acknowledge and say thank you to Joannah Saxton and Susan Miller for their help in the preparation of the manuscript for *Choosing to Learn from Life*. Finally, I want to thank all the folks at Cook Communications for everything they have done to make this book possible.

—MIKE BREEN

Meet the Authors

MIKE BREEN

As rector and team leader of St. Thomas' Church in Sheffield, Mike used *LifeShapes* to grow the largest church in the north of England, with more than two thousand attending weekly worship and 80 percent of the congregation under age forty. The church became known for its deep spiritual growth and authentic community.

Mike spent the better part of a decade developing this visually oriented teaching tool. *LifeShapes* proved its effectiveness among the members of this largely twenty- and thirty-something congregation. Helping them not only to understand biblical principles on a deeper level, but also to apply those principles to their lives. St. Thomas' Church became a church passionate to know Christ and make him known.

Mike now teaches at Fuller Theological Seminary in Pasadena, California, and serves on staff at Community Church of Joy in Glendale, Arizona. He also travels the country teaching the concepts of *LifeShapes*, introduced to people in the United States in Mike's recent books *The Passionate Church* and *A Passionate Life*. He helps church leaders in transition and coaches church planters to be effective in our contemporary culture—and helps the church itself to reflect the foundation of its name: community.

Mike lives in Phoenix, Arizona, with his wife, Sally, and their son, Sam. He has two daughters currently living in the United Kingdom.

MAL CALLADINE

Mal Calladine had a powerful encounter with Jesus at age eighteen. One year later, he met Mike Breen while attending college at Oxford. After attending Mike's church for about two years (at that time, Mike was the pastor of All Saints Church, Streatham Hill in Brixton, London), Mal began praying about pursuing a position in church ministry. He went to Mike for advice and came away with a job offer.

That first step toward ministry leadership began a fifteen-year journey of exploring the edges of what church could be like. After working with Mike for a season, Mal worked for Anglican Church Planting Initiatives and then for St. Andrew's Chorleywood. He eventually made his way to Sheffield. Visiting the local parish (located within five hundred yards of his home), Mal was shocked to find that Mike Breen had become the church leader there.

Having first learned the concept of the Circle while working with Mike in London, Mal now had the opportunity to fully absorb its impact on his life. He spent the next seven years learning *LifeShapes* inside and out.

Today Mal lives with his wife and three children in Charleston, South Carolina, where he serves on the leadership team of St. Andrew's Church, teaching and applying the principles of *LifeShapes*.

God! Please Do Something!

I had been ordained as a minister in the Church of England for two years, serving as a curate (like an assistant pastor) and then leading a youth ministry in the local town. I was young and naive, full of drive and determination. God had called me to win souls for the kingdom, and that was exactly what I was going to do. I was invincible. As time passed, I began to get a taste of the real world, and suddenly I was struck with the realization that things weren't going all that well. Nothing was going according to the hopes and dreams I had for my ministry. I had signed up to change the world for Christ, but so far no one had become a Christian as a result of my ministry. I'd preached my heart out, expecting results that would rival the great evangelistic stories of the New Testament. Yet I'm not sure anyone remembered what I said by the time they were eating lunch.

I did the best I could. Nothing was happening. Talk about disappointment and a feeling of failure. Everything I had planned, everything I had prayed for lay shattered at my feet in a heap of broken expectations. By that time, I wasn't at all certain of what God wanted from my life, and I felt ill-equipped to get myself to that point. I had spent many hours contemplating with the Lord the future of my ministry.

Then one day, a young woman who sat at the back of church

spoke to my wife, Sally, and me at the end of the service.

"I think I'd like to find out about Christianity."

Yes! Finally things were moving! I was so excited. We met with her for dinner several times in the following weeks and led her through a booklet that explained what it was to become a Christian. And she did, in fact, become a Christian. Yes! This was the start of great things; I was sure of it. The church would grow. My ministry would flourish.

To my disappointment, the young woman soon left our church and joined another one!

I was devastated.

Life muddled along without much success in my ministry, at least as I would have defined it. One sunny afternoon in August, I was in the backyard, going through my usual conversation with God, saying, "Lord, what is wrong with me? I thought I'd done everything you wanted ..." when I came across some ant nests. Rebecca, our firstborn child, had just learned how to walk. These were the kind of ants that would bite—and eat Rebecca alive if I didn't prevent it. Not my baby! Much as I love all God's creatures, these ants had to die.

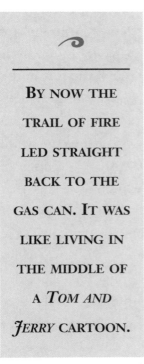

By now the trail of fire led straight back to the gas can. It was like living in the middle of a *Tom and Jerry* cartoon.

So I thought to myself, *Now what would my dad do about these ants?* The obvious answer jumped right out: *Burn them!*

God bless my father, but maybe this indicates the kind of gene pool I come out of. When I asked Dad later, he said, "Yeah, I probably would have done the same thing."

So, I went to the garage, got a rather large can of gasoline, returned to the backyard, and generously poured it all around. Now, remember, it's the middle of August, so the gasoline is rapidly turning to vapor in the surrounding air. I put the can down and returned to the house for matches. I couldn't find a match anywhere. To this day I think there were angels all over the house, calling to each other, saying, "Stop him now! Hide the matches!"

But I am persistent when it comes to keeping my children safe. Leaving no drawer unopened and no pile unturned, I found some matches and went back into the yard.

Do you know that you don't even have to throw the match into the puddles of gasoline? It's amazing; all you have to do is strike one. The ants were gone, instantly swallowed up in the incineration. Mission accomplished, or so I thought. However, as I looked around, I realized that I had one small problem. The whole yard was on fire!

By now the trail of fire led straight back to the gas can. It was like living in the middle of a *Tom and Jerry* cartoon. Can't you just see it—a trail of fire roaring toward a gas can. You know what's going to happen, but somehow the cartoon characters don't. Well, I knew what was going to happen. I just didn't figure it out fast enough. I had just walked around the yard, pouring gasoline wherever I went, just in case there were Rebecca-attacking ants elsewhere in the yard, leaving a path of liquid fuel straight back to the can.

When the spout of the gas can caught on fire, I thought, *That's a bomb.* I could see tomorrow's headlines

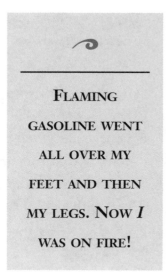

FLAMING GASOLINE WENT ALL OVER MY FEET AND THEN MY LEGS. NOW *I* WAS ON FIRE!

in the local paper: "Crater Found in Pastor's Backyard (Still Looking for Pastor)." My next thought was, *The thing to do is get the can away from the source of heat.* So I leaned across and picked up the can. It was hot. Really hot. On-fire hot. I dropped the can.

Until then, I had never built a flamethrower. Let me share with you the rather easy flamethrower-building technique I learned that fateful day:

1. Get a can full of gas. Make sure it has a spout.
2. Light the spout with a match.
3. Eject the contents of the can through the spout. Simply dropping the can onto the ground works just as well.

Unfortunately on that August day the flamethrower was aimed in my direction. Flaming gasoline went all over my feet and then my legs. Now *I* was on fire!

In those few split seconds I considered the options given in those safety films that instruct you about what to do in the event you catch fire:

OPTION #1: ROLL AROUND ON THE GROUND.

The ground was on fire so that was not going to do me any good at all.

OPTION #2: GET SOMEONE TO WRAP A BLANKET AROUND YOU.

There was not a soul in that yard with a blanket! Sally was my only hope, and she was out walking the dog.

I could do only one thing—take my pants off.

My religious training ran strong and deep. Running around the backyard with no pants was just not a Christian thing to do. I didn't want to take my pants off! Instead, I kicked off my shoe, which was also on fire, sending it into the next-door neighbor's yard. (Its charred remains were returned to us later by a very confused neighbor.)

Oddly enough, throwing a flaming shoe didn't really help anything. The pants still had to go. I was about to take my pants down when I looked up to heaven and cried, "God! Please do something!" When I looked down again, the flames were out! Then, as you do in these situations, I breathed a sigh of relief, said, "Boy, that was close," and walked back into the house.

Sally had come home by now, and she immediately asked, "What is that smell?" Not much gets past Sally.

"Oh, just had a little accident," I explained. "A few ants, a match, and some gasoline ..."

"What! What have you done?"

"Well ... I just ... kind of ... set fire to myself ... a little bit. It's no big deal; it's fine. I'll make myself a cup of tea." A typical Englishman: Make yourself a cup of tea and everything is fine!

Sally wouldn't let it go. She's that way.

"Let me have a look at your legs."

"But they're fine!"

"Let me have a look at your legs, Mike."

So there in the kitchen, I took my pants down. Huge folds of skin hung off my legs. I thought, *Wow, I bet that's going to be painful when it starts to hurt.*

Sally got me in the car and rushed me to the emergency room. As soon as we arrived, the pain hit me. I had third-degree burns on my legs. Very soon they were infected. The doctors put me in an isolation unit. I couldn't see anyone except for the briefest of visits. I couldn't even hold my daughter. The only exception to this rule was the nurse whose sole purpose in life was to come in two or three times a day to inflict pain on me when she took the bandages off to see how my legs were doing and to wrap them back up again. It was awful.

I was desperate, lonely, and depressed, feelings I was not used to experiencing.

During that time, I had no one else to talk to except God, and the cry of my heart began to emerge. I began to question what I was doing and where I was going with my life.

"God! Please do something!"

And his reply was very simple: *Well, let me do it.*

In other words, *I'm better at it than you are, so learn how to get out of the way. Learn to be the channel for me, rather than a representative that just does stuff for me. Let me do it.*

God was using the difficulty and pain of my situation to turn me around and change my life. He had to get me alone and at a standstill before he could get through to answer my questions; but through the books I read, the tapes I listened to, the prayers I prayed, I felt God saying the same thing again and again.

Let me do it.

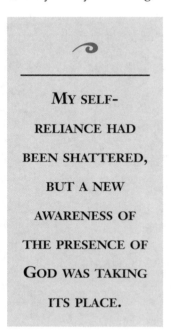

MY SELF-RELIANCE HAD BEEN SHATTERED, BUT A NEW AWARENESS OF THE PRESENCE OF GOD WAS TAKING ITS PLACE.

As I recovered in the hospital, I realized that a major change was taking place. My self-reliance had been shattered, but a new awareness of the presence of God was taking its place. My relationship with God was being renewed.

When I returned to work, an old friend invited me to lead a youth retreat. I had led many retreats in the past, but with God saying he wanted control this time, I didn't know what to do.

Every session we led was like scaling a rock wall for me. I was fearful, inarticulate, and not particularly entertaining, yet God seemed to be doing something. By the last session I was so scared I trembled at the mere thought of going into the room. But I went. I gave a simple message based on the cross of Jesus and what he had achieved there. Many were moved at the time, but it wasn't until much later I discovered from my friend that God had come in power. Most of the young people became Christians or rededicated their lives to Christ within twenty-four hours of the last session. Some of those young people are in ministry today.

I didn't really understand what had happened, and I definitely had no method or program of repeating the experience. It was over the days and months that followed that a learning process or method of discipleship began to emerge. In seminary, Mike Williams, my lecturer in pastoral theology, introduced our class to a four-stage learning process symbolized by a circle. It was similar to a method of planning and review that was (and still is) common in modern business and management theory. In the subsequent years of learning how to let God control my life and ministry, I found the image of the Learning Circle a helpful tool in understanding the process God led me through in the big and small events of my life. As I searched the Scriptures, particularly the life of Jesus, and reflected on God's workings in my life, I discovered six stages of the process of learning to let God have his way in my life.

And so the process I describe as the Learning Circle was born, not on the mountaintops of ministry, but in one of the deepest valleys of my life.

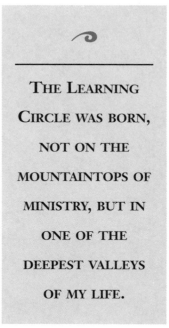

THE LEARNING CIRCLE WAS BORN, NOT ON THE MOUNTAINTOPS OF MINISTRY, BUT IN ONE OF THE DEEPEST VALLEYS OF MY LIFE.

I began to discover how to let God come into my life and lead the way. I have simply tried to do what Jesus did, and allow his principles to become the framework for following him—the new structure of a passionate life.

CHAPTER 1

From Desperation to Passion

*H*ave you ever cried out to God in sheer desperation?

Hopefully you weren't setting yourself on fire like I was. But you may have felt the same depth and urgency of desperation. You can't take this situation one minute longer. It's going to swallow you up as sure as gasoline bursts into flames. "God! Please do something!"

I'd been stuck in a rut for some time when I set myself on fire. And the longer I stayed in that place, the more desperate I became. While I don't recommend setting fire to a can of gasoline in your backyard, clearly that event was the catalyst for God to begin changing me—and for me to be ready to let him do it.

What is your point of desperation? Perhaps for you it's your marriage. You love your spouse, but some issues never seem to get resolved—the same argument rears its head on an almost predictable schedule. You both want it to be different, but somehow it just never is. There you are, back in that loop once again, saying things that don't help anything except to make you feel vindicated. The buttons get hotter and hotter, so to avoid hitting them, you drift apart.

IT SEEMS WE KNOW A LOT ABOUT PREPARING FOR LIFE; WE JUST DON'T KNOW HOW TO LIVE OUR LIVES, HOW TO REALLY LIVE.

Or maybe you're struggling under the pressure of a crippling financial burden. You may have gotten yourself into debt way over your head. You bought a big new house, you took a vacation you couldn't really afford, and you convinced yourself you needed a new SUV even if it meant a seven-year loan. The reasons for your debt may be beyond your control—serious illness in the family with astronomical medical bills, losing a job you didn't even know was in peril—but the debt is crushing all the same. "Get out of debt" is a New Year's resolution you make in January only to give up on in February.

Maybe there is an issue with sin that is dragging you down—a temptation you keep giving in to even though you've determined again and again to change. Your temptation may be a serious addiction, selfishness, pride, or a tendency to overindulge in chocolate. You've tried to change, you've prayed for change, but no lasting change has come into your life in this particular area. In fact, the temptation is as strong as it ever was, and you are just as likely to succumb as you ever were. Ultimately, you feel trapped in an endless cycle of attempts to change followed by failure.

Spiritual discipline, family relationships, ministry life, and work challenges—we all have areas of life where it seems that some things never change no matter how hard we try. We seem to be doomed to revisiting the same life lessons over and over again. Whatever we've been doing it's not working, because there is no lasting change. Surely this is not the life God intended for us!

WHAT'S THE SECRET?

Ever feel like everyone knows the secret to living a meaningful life except you? Not everyone has an overwhelming issue or a haunting situation. Maybe you just want to know how to "do" life in a more significant way, a way that brings you joy, a way that leaves you satisfied at the end of the day. You're not alone. Just look around you—more and more people are spending more and more time, money, and energy trying to get "ready" for life. There are 1–2–3 lists for how to prepare for a certain career path, courses to equip you with the right skills to propel you to the top of any profession, life coaches who promise to empower you for a more fulfilling life. It seems we know a lot about preparing for life; we just don't know how to live our lives, how to really live.

A study of the current generation of young adults can shine a light on what our culture is teaching us about living. *Time* magazine ran an article about "Twixters,"[1] the phenomenon referring to America's young adults who seemingly are caught between adolescence and adulthood. The *Time* article stated that, when it came to living in the real world, 19 percent of young adults felt that school did not actually prepare them to be successful in their work life. In addition, the ability or inability to make career decisions among the Twixters spills over into their personal lives as well. It's not that the Twixters aren't taking adulthood seriously. Rather, they take it *so* seriously that they spend years choosing just the right path into it.

---

1. Lev Grossman, "Grow Up? Not So Fast," *Time* 165, no. 4 (January 24, 2005), p. 42.

They are immobilized in their pursuit to find the right answers to all their questions:

- How do I have a happy and fulfilling marriage?
- How do I raise healthy and secure children?
- How do I learn to work with that difficult colleague?
- How do I stop making the same mistakes in my relationships, finances, and career again and again?
- How do I change, really change?

Carter Duryea is a classic fictional example of a Twixter. The film *In Good Company*[2] tells the story of Duryea (played by Topher Grace), a twenty-six-year-old whiz kid of a multinational conglomerate, GLOBECOM. His promotion to the head of the ad sales department of GLOBECOM's latest acquisition, *Sports America* magazine, coincides

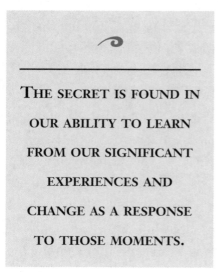

THE SECRET IS FOUND IN OUR ABILITY TO LEARN FROM OUR SIGNIFICANT EXPERIENCES AND CHANGE AS A RESPONSE TO THOSE MOMENTS.

with the disintegration of his seven-month marriage. Duryea is being groomed for greatness in his career, yet in reality he is lonely, insecure, and unprepared for all that life brings. The only way he knows to learn from life is to learn from his mistakes—the hard way.

At the close of the film, Duryea loses his position and decides to start over. But before he leaves, he thanks his colleague Dan Foreman (played by Dennis Quaid) and makes a profound admission: No one had ever cared

---

2. Paul Weitz, *In Good Company*, DVD, directed by Paul Weitz (Hollywood, Calif.: Universal, 2004).

enough to give him a hard time before or to teach him the things he *really* needed to know about life. No one had taught him what he needed to know most—how to learn from life while he's living it.

Life's answers don't always live in the amount of knowledge we can accumulate. The secret is found in our ability to learn from our significant experiences and change as a response to those moments. Jesus will show you how.

LEARN FROM ME

As we read the books and watch the television shows of our culture, we soon see that we are not isolated in our desire to learn how to live our lives to the fullest. The rise of "reality shows" points out the desperate search for meaning and happiness. Contestants go on these shows to be better dressers, better spouses, better parents, and richer people. They want to be winners of whatever competition they face, whether it is finding romance on ABC's *The Bachelor*, traveling around the world faster than anyone else on NBC's *The Amazing Race*, or eating more gross organisms than anyone else on NBC's *Fear Factor*. Shows like NBC's *Starting Over* give women the opportunity to address their lives and take steps that will produce permanent change. Professional nannies swoop into your home to help you get control of unruly children.

Today's talk shows overflow with experts who want to fix your life: psychologists, life coaches, celebrity hosts, financial experts, writers. People go on the shows and bare their souls to a national audience and come home "fixed." Or they watch other people do this and line up the similarities with their own lives, casting about for tidbits of advice they can apply.

For some of us, when it comes to a full life, we don't try to get fixed. Instead, we want to escape. We watch sports on TV, remembering our high school or college days and the unfulfilled potential of the past. Or we identify ourselves with our current foot- ball, baseball, or basketball heroes, and their success becomes our suc- cess. Or we engage in the world of computer games. Opportunities to control the universe, defeat aliens, battle evil empires, or become sport- ing legends lay at our fingertips. We get to live the kind of life heroes live; we get to be the hero! It's a world away from a life that we can do nothing about and where cir- cumstances never seem to change.

> THE QUESTION IS NOT ONE OF KNOWLEDGE, BUT OF APPLICATION. BUT WE CAN'T ADMIT THAT, CAN WE?

As Christians, we are expected to go to our churches and small groups, looking for answers. "Jesus is the answer." With our heads, we believe that. Experientially, though, we have a much harder time figuring out what that means on a day-to-day basis. How is Jesus the answer when that familiar quarrel comes around yet again? How is Jesus the answer when the bottom falls out of the big project at work? How is Jesus the answer when a difficult child frays at the garment of your family life? The question is not one of knowledge, but of application. But we can't admit that, can we? We can't let fellow believers know that we haven't figured out how to apply the only true answer. So we carry on, wondering, frustrated, disappointed, and living in the shadow of the passionate life that Jesus offers but that we have rarely experienced.

There is good news! Listen to these words from Jesus:

> Come to me, all you who are weary and burdened, and I will give you rest. Take my yoke upon you and

learn from me, for I am gentle and humble in heart, and you will find rest for your souls. For my yoke is easy and my burden is light.

—Matthew 11:28–30

The One whom we know to be the Answer offers us an invitation. "Learn from me." For those of us who are weary of the repetitive patterns of our lives, the ruts we are stuck in, the inability to make decisions and work through circumstances of life, there is hope: Learn from Jesus.

CHECK YOUR TOOL BELT

The Learning Circle helps us learn the way in which Jesus taught his disciples how to understand the world. We learn from their experience. When it comes to our own experiences, we don't automatically learn simply because we have experiences. We learn by intentionally choosing to learn. We learn by choosing to enter the Circle.

Like all of the eight *LifeShapes* tools, the Learning Circle is a tool that is meant to be both memorable and repeatable. It's a tool that you can pull out and use in many different situations, just as if you had a hammer and screwdriver hanging from your belt. If you don't wear your tool belt, you start to think you don't need it. You forget about the tools that could be right at your fingertips and try to do things the hard way—and probably end up hurting yourself in the process! But if you wear your tool belt, you're constantly reaching for just the right tool to make things easier.

It's the same with *LifeShapes* tools. If you carry them around in your head and your heart, you'll be amazed at how many times you find yourself reaching for them. And when you draw around you others who carry the same tools, you'll find you develop a simple language for encouraging one another to make the right choices.

If you have read *The Passionate Church* or *A Passionate Life* or gone through *A Passionate Life* as a small-group study, these next few chapters will be a very helpful review of the Learning Circle for you. We're going to cover the basic application of the Circle and give scriptural examples of how people in the Bible lived the Circle. But it doesn't stop there. We will also explore the depths of each step of the Circle in such a way that you will be left feeling like you can take this material, apply the ideas and principles to the situations of your own life, and begin to disciple others to do the same.

As you begin to learn and grow from your Circle experiences, you will no doubt encounter many successes and many failures. Let me encourage you with this: If it's worth doing, it's worth doing poorly. That's right—you may do it poorly at first. Don't let that stop you, or you will never learn to do it well. One of the best ways of learning how to do *LifeShapes* well in your own life is to teach others what you have learned. Even if you don't know every nook and cranny of *LifeShapes* or fully understand the principles, come forward with a humble heart, and lead others in this journey with you.

And now, we invite you to spend some time on your journey with us. Maybe you've put your frustrating situation on the shelf. Perhaps in your fear of being disappointed yet again, you have come to expect less from God when it comes to changing your life. Perhaps you can't see how anything could change your marriage, your job, your family, and you—not now. Join us in this journey around the Learning Circle. In response to our cry of "God, please do something!" Jesus teaches us how to learn from life. Let's see how the Lord meets us there.

Are you ready to learn?

CHAPTER 2

When Time Stands Still

Key Words

Chronos *Time:*
The sequential passing of time, chronological time.
It's about dates and clock time.

Kairos *Time:*
An event, moment, or crisis when time can seem to "stand still."
A period of "time" when chronos *is of no importance.*
It could mark a significant shift in your life.

*T*iberius is ruler of the expansive Roman Empire, including Palestine, populated by Jewish people. Out of the wilderness, the voice of John the Baptist begins calling people to another kingdom—the kingdom of God. He preaches that the kingdom of God is near, so people had better get ready! This kingdom would not be the political kingdom the Jews had longed for, but a rule of righteousness. Being part of this kingdom requires a whole new way of thinking—it requires repentance.

Rome is not concerned in the least. The emperor has bigger problems—like trying to survive the deadly betrayal and infighting of the dynasty of Caesar. John the Baptist is an eccentric who is not worth a glance from Tiberius.

On the other hand, Jewish leaders are getting a little restless. What is this fringe prophet talking about? It is one thing to expect Gentiles to be baptized if they want to believe in the Jewish God, but it is another to expect Jews to be baptized as a sign of repentance.

One day Jesus shows up at the Jordan River, and things get even more complicated. John recognizes Jesus as one who is greater than he is—the one the Jews have been waiting for. Yet Jesus asks John to baptize him. When that happens, the voice of God speaks. This is a history-changing moment. John knows that his ministry of preparing the way is coming to a close, because the real thing is here. The kingdom has arrived. As Jesus' own public ministry gets under way, he moves from saying that the kingdom is "near" to "the kingdom has come."

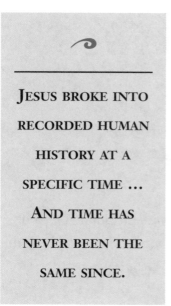

JESUS BROKE INTO RECORDED HUMAN HISTORY AT A SPECIFIC TIME ... AND TIME HAS NEVER BEEN THE SAME SINCE.

Later, in prison for denouncing the immoral behavior of the Jewish leader Herod Antipas, John is discouraged. He seeks affirmation by sending two of his followers to ask Jesus if he really is the Messiah. Jesus responds by pointing out his miracles and preaching that fulfilled the Old Testament prophets. Though shortly after this event John is beheaded, he is able to face his death knowing that his ministry is complete—the kingdom of God truly has come.

Jesus broke into recorded human history at a specific time and in a specific place. He was not a theoretical religious figure. He walked the roads of Galilee and Judea; he had relationships with the people around him; he paid his taxes; he read Scripture in the synagogue. And time has never been the same since.

While John is in prison, Jesus goes to Galilee, the most northern district of Palestine. Galilee was known to have incredibly fertile land, more than anywhere else in Palestine. "Galilee" comes from a Hebrew word meaning *a circle*. The full name of the region was Galilee of the Gentiles. Surrounded by Gentiles, Galilee's history was one of constant struggle as surrounding nations sought to dominate the area. By Jesus' time, Galilee's great roads led out to all over the known world. It wasn't a large area, but it overflowed with people. Perhaps as a result of their history, Galileans were known to be courageous people, but also fertile ground for new ideas. It was the ideal place to share a new and radical message and watch it spread.

Jesus begins his ministry with a very short sermon—a sermon that is the summary statement of all his teaching and ideas for the coming few years. This message sets the stage for all he is about to say and do.

> After John was put in prison, Jesus went into Galilee,
> proclaiming the good news of God. "The time has
> come," he said. "The kingdom of God is near. Repent
> and believe the good news!"
> —Mark 1:14–15

Jesus says to his listeners that a great opportunity is available to them; God's kingdom is within reach! However, taking hold of this amazing opportunity involves a process of repentance and belief.

Now to both the courageous Galileans and to us today, such an offer may seem exciting, challenging, inspirational, and intriguing all at the same time.

But what exactly is Jesus talking about? What does he mean?

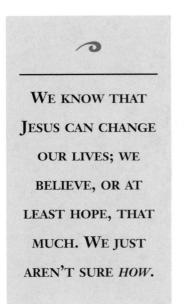

WE KNOW THAT JESUS CAN CHANGE OUR LIVES; WE BELIEVE, OR AT LEAST HOPE, THAT MUCH. WE JUST AREN'T SURE *HOW*.

In these sentences we discover how Jesus helped his disciples understand the world and to learn from their experiences. So this message is at the heart of the Learning Circle.

If these words are the definitive message that explains the opportunity that knowing Christ presents, then it's worth taking the time to dig a little deeper to understand what Jesus is saying to us. We know that Jesus can change our lives; we believe, or at least hope, that much. We just aren't sure *how*.

How can we learn to see that change takes place in the ordinary events of life on a regular basis? If we are going to respond to the words of Jesus when he says, "Learn from me" (Matt. 11:28–30), then we need to look at four words in this message in Mark 1. It contains some powerful insights that are keys to living a passionate life.

Time

Kingdom

Repent

Believe

WHAT "TIME" IS IT?

In English, we have the word "time," and we use it many different ways. Greek, the original language of the New Testament, has many words for time with specific meanings.

Chronos is the kind of time that is sequential, calendar time, wristwatch time. *Chronos* is the kind of time we would use in the question, "What time is it?" or, "What time do you think the preacher is going to finish tonight?" It's the kind of time where you're conscious of the sequence of ongoing time, how long something takes.

Kairos is completely different. *Kairos* is event time, crisis time, the kind of time we would use in the statement, "That was a great time last night," or "Didn't we have a good time the other day? What a time that was!" You are not aware of the clock when it's *kairos* time. In that moment time seems to stand still.

Sometimes *kairos* time marks a significant situation in your life. That's the kind of time, *kairos* time, that Jesus speaks of in Mark 1:14–15.

Jesus tells the Galileans that the event they had been awaiting for generations had finally arrived. For centuries, they had been invaded and oppressed by other nations. Even during the time of Jesus they were under Roman occupation. The Jews of this generation had never known freedom, but they held on to the promise that God would send someone to save them, to rescue them.

When Jesus proclaims in Galilee, "The time has come," he is saying, *An event has occurred; the lines of expectation and prophecy in the Old Testament have come together and this is* kairos; *this is the event you want; this is the opportunity you have been waiting for. God has sent the Messiah to save his people.*

This is significant!

HAS TIME EVER STOOD STILL FOR YOU?

Think of some of the significant events that have taken place in your life. These were *kairos* events.

Kairos events can either be negative or positive experiences. They can be times of celebration and joy or times of pain and sadness.

When you think of your wedding day, you probably don't recall how long it took to say your vows, but it was definitely an event when time stood still: *kairos* time.

The birth of your children—didn't they all tell you life would never be the same? *Kairos*.

That promotion at work brought a significant shift in how you and your family live: *kairos*.

Think of a family vacation—perhaps time stood still then? Maybe you wish it hadn't—we did say that a *kairos* wasn't *always* positive!

KAIROS LEAVES ITS MARK

Some *kairos* events mark our lives because of the pain they bring: The death of a loved one—you remember when you heard the news and how the words hung ominously in the air. When they finally landed, your world changed forever.

Signing those divorce papers, confirming that the end had arrived, learning that you would be "let go" at work—time stood still, didn't it?

That's one way of recognizing that you have entered *kairos* time: The event leaves an impact on you—and it's never neutral. When it came to the World Series, October 27, 2004, was a *kairos* event for both the fans of the Boston Red Sox and the St. Louis Cardinals, but in very different ways. For Red Sox fans, an eighty-six-year wait was finally over and they would savor the moment!

It was time to celebrate! Cardinals fans felt an entirely different emotion. Their team had gotten so far, but not far enough. It was over.

Whether good or bad, big or small, *kairos* events make an impression on us.

When we look for them, we realize *kairos* events take place everywhere! We go to a restaurant, and it is a great time or an awful time. We're sitting at the intersection, and we look at the wrong set of lights. We think they're green, we move, and then we realize the mistake. We have a near miss on the freeway. We have an argument or a challenge in our lives, and it causes us some kind of crisis. We have wonderful times; we have hard times.

It could be in your family life or the politics of the office. It could be something that takes place in the life of your church. It could happen in your recreational time, playing a round of golf, spending time in conversation with friends. And although they vary in their significance, we experience *kairos* events every single day.

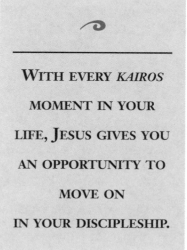

WITH EVERY *KAIROS* MOMENT IN YOUR LIFE, JESUS GIVES YOU AN OPPORTUNITY TO MOVE ON IN YOUR DISCIPLESHIP.

As we learn to recognize *kairos* events, the next step is to figure out what we're supposed to do with them.

Perhaps many of us file them away in the back of our minds and ignore them, even forget them. When a *kairos* event produces a positive effect, we hope and pray that life stays that way forever, sometimes even trying to relive the moment again and again to recapture the great feelings. When a *kairos* event produces a negative effect, we may focus on what led up to that moment in the hope of preventing it from happening again.

Or there's another path we could take.

Jesus said to those who were listening to his message the first time that *kairos* presents an *opportunity*. With every *kairos* moment in your life, Jesus gives you an opportunity to move on in your discipleship. It's a great opportunity for you to grow as a person; it's a wonderful opportunity for you to step into the process of learning the way Jesus teaches us to learn. It's an opportunity for God to intervene and for you to learn from Jesus.

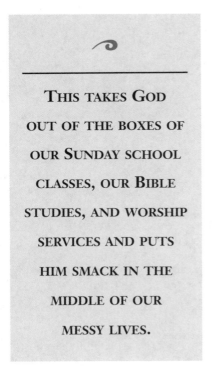

THIS TAKES GOD OUT OF THE BOXES OF OUR SUNDAY SCHOOL CLASSES, OUR BIBLE STUDIES, AND WORSHIP SERVICES AND PUTS HIM SMACK IN THE MIDDLE OF OUR MESSY LIVES.

The time has come. The kingdom of God is near. But what is the "kingdom" of God, and what does it look like for us living today? The next chapter explores the ideas of "kingdom," but let me begin by saying this: The kingdom of God is the fulfillment of all human hopes and aspirations. Everything we could wish for finds its fulfillment in our relationship with God.

In other words, when we encounter these *kairos* events, whether they are positive or negative, it's as though the curtain between the kingdom of God and the kingdom of this world is pulled back a little bit. It's as though the margin between the two worlds gets thinner, narrower. It's as though you can push through. Jesus seems to be saying that the kingdom is so close that you could reach out with one hand and take it—that's why some of the translations say, "The kingdom of God is at hand."

•••••••••••••••• X •••••••••••••••► **Kingdom**

So when you go through these experiences, it's as though the Lord wants each of us to learn how to make the most of this event, so that we can enter afresh into his kingdom and to receive anew what it means to grow in him.

Now before we go on to explore what the kingdom looks like and how God fulfills all our present hopes and aspirations, we need to realize that this is *good news*. God wants to impact every single part of our lives. This takes God out of the boxes of our Sunday school classes, our Bible studies, and worship services and puts him smack in the middle of our messy lives. And that's exactly where he wants to be.

When you argue with that boss, when that business deal falls through, God is near.

When you fight with your spouse repeatedly and you have little hope, God is near.

When you get promoted at work, God is near.

When your teen slams the door in your face and you don't know what to do next, God is near.

When your children are born.

When you struggle with singleness.

When you start out in married life.

When you experience devastating loss.

When you experience crushing disappointment.

When you realize that you are bored with life.

When life is going really well or when you know it's just not working, God is near.

It's an opportunity to grow, to experience the kingdom of God.

Think of a *kairos* you are going through right now. God is right there with you. You have an opportunity to simply reach out with your life and enter into his kingdom. Once there, you can begin to experience, right here on earth, the life-changing power of living in God's presence.

CHAPTER 3

The Return of the King

Key Word

Kingdom:
The rule of God in our lives, his kingship.
It does not refer to a geographical location.
The kingdom refers to God's effective and powerful presence
and influence in our lives.

A four-year-old boy finds a loaded gun under his parents' dresser. Bang! Bang! He shoots his two-year-old sibling.

In Israel, a nineteen-year-old man boards a bus knowing he won't get off. No one will. In a few minutes it blows up. The suicide bomber has lived out his destiny.

A fourteen-year-old girl goes missing from her family for more than a year, snatched against her will by cultish religious fanatics.

Four prisoners kill a guard and escape, armed and dangerous.

In Iraq, innocent children are maimed and killed by bombs set by their own people.

A CEO of a major corporation manipulates the books. He makes a fortune. Stockholders lose their retirement money.

This is the stuff of daily newscasts. We get a snack during the commercials and come back to hear the five-day weather forecast and the sports.

How did the world get to such a state that events like these are routine—and we barely feel their impact?

Once upon a time, humanity was in perfect relationship with God. God clearly established a pattern of walking "in the cool of the day" (Gen. 3:8 KJV) with Adam and Eve. They had complete intimacy with God and a healthy and whole relationship with each other. Enter the Serpent, the physical representation of Satan. He deceived Adam and Eve into making a choice that disrupted their intimacy with God. They fell to a place far below what they were used to, and we are all born into that place.

The old world is lost and has fallen into chaos, rebellion, and under the tyranny of the god of this world, the thief who came to kill and steal and destroy. We see the effects of that fallen, broken world every day—because it's *our* world. We see it on the news, in our communities, in our places of work, and in our family lives.

Yet God, in his infinite mercy and grace, decided to create a whole new world in which humanity can again be in the same state of grace that existed in Eden. Even now, God is making a kingdom for all humanity. His intention, through Jesus, is to save us from the separation of sin and bring us into a new kingdom he is preparing.

A SEAM OF GOLD

The theme of the kingdom of God runs through the Bible like a seam of gold. In the eighth century BC, Isaiah said, "My eyes have seen the King, the LORD Almighty" (Isa. 6:5). This same prophet spoke of the "son of David" appointed by God and prophesied that a Messiah would come in the future and take the throne of David. Obadiah and Zechariah declared that one day God would rule over the whole earth and that all people would worship him. Daniel painted a vivid picture of the fall of world empires and the rule of the Most High. The era of the Evil One will end, and the kingdom of God will take over.

In the Gospels, we hear Jesus speaking of the kingdom of God over and over, in his sermons, in his parables and by his miracles. Jesus doesn't teach about a geographical kingdom, to which we can swear allegiance. His message is all about the rule of God. It's coming and we'd better be ready! The story of the unexpected burglar in Matthew 24:42–44, the sudden arrival of the bridegroom in Matthew 25:1–13, and many other stories are pictures of the arrival of God's kingdom. It will come that quickly and change our lives that radically.

When we think of the kingdom of God, perhaps many of us think of heaven. And that is right—that's exactly where we are heading. Jesus spoke of the kingdom of God as being a future reality. The book of Revelation says this:

> And I heard a loud voice from the throne saying,
> "Now the dwelling of God is with men, and he will
> live with them. They will be his people, and God him-
> self will be with them and be their God. He will wipe
> every tear from their eyes. There will be no more
> death or mourning or crying or pain, for the old order
> of things has passed away." He who was seated on the
> throne said, "I am making everything new!"
> —Revelation 21:3–5

A PRESENT KINGDOM

But Jesus doesn't leave the kingdom of God in the future. He wraps it up within himself. He casts out demons, he heals miraculously, and he disarms Satan, because the kingdom is not only coming, it's here! In Jesus, the future rule of God breaks into the present moment. Through Jesus, the heavenly sense of bounty and fulfillment we know our lives will have can be experienced right now, today! The power of the kingdom is undeniable. We know how the story will end—God will win the battle against evil—and we're drawn into the plot to experience all the excitement from the inside.

THE KINGDOM IS NOT ONLY COMING—IT'S HERE! IN JESUS, THE FUTURE RULE OF GOD BREAKS INTO THE PRESENT MOMENT.

Jesus enters the stage of world history with the kingdom of God as his central message. The tyranny of the god of this broken, fallen world meant that people were enslaved by sin, by sickness, by sadness, and by Satan himself. So what does Jesus do? Because Jesus is God—the King—he not only speaks of the kingdom, but he brings with him realities of the kingdom. In his words, his relationships, his actions, and ultimately through his death and resurrection, he defeats Satan once and for all.

Jesus heals sickness. He speaks with authority like no one else. He is master over the laws of nature and science. Demons scream out at him, "What do you want with us, Son of God?" and he casts them out and brings wholeness to suffering people. He announces in the synagogue that he is the fulfillment of Isaiah's prophecy.

When the friends of a paralytic bring the man to Jesus, he does more than heal his legs—he forgives the man's sins. He tells his closest disciples that he would die so that the "prince of this world will be driven out" (John 12:31). And in his death, lifted up on the cross, he would draw all people to himself and to the Father.

But what does the kingdom look like for those of us living today? To be honest, it looks exactly as it did two thousand years ago when Jesus first revealed it. The very presence of Jesus in our lives means that the future kingdom of God is revealed to us right now. John 14:27 is just as true today as it was then: "Peace I leave with you; my peace I give you." Jesus has given us a taste of his kingdom through the personal peace granted to us in our relationship with him. In the future kingdom, there is no death (Rev. 21:4), and upon our acceptance of Christ's salvation, we are granted eternal life (John 3:16). Our freedom from death and separation does not begin when we enter into the future kingdom; it has already begun. We are living in the kingdom right now! Just as there is no sickness in heaven and just as surely as Jesus healed the sick when he walked the earth, he continues to heal people from sickness and disease today. That is God's kingdom breaking into the present.

Now this is good news! The reality that God has made—

> THIS IS WHAT WE PRAY FOR WHEN WE SAY, "YOUR KINGDOM COME." WE ARE ASKING FOR GOD'S RULE TO BREAK INTO OUR LIVES, TO INFLUENCE THE WORLD IN WHICH WE LIVE, AND TO BRING US THE REALITY OF HEAVEN.

heaven—breaks into our reality. It's as though the future bursts into our lives and leaves it mark. This is what we pray for when we say, "Your kingdom come." We are asking for God's rule to break into our lives, to influence the world in which we live, and to bring us the reality of heaven, where there is no sin, sickness, sadness, or the influence of Satan as part of our daily lives.

In the last chapter, I said that the kingdom of God is the fulfillment of all human hopes and aspirations. In the context of our relationship with God, this means that God has allowed us to experience moments in our life on earth that will be eternal moments in the future kingdom. Moments of peace, moments of health, moments of bounty and blessing. And as we learn to process those moments, learn from those moments, and live intimately with Christ in those moments, we move another step closer to the kingdom.

This is dramatic stuff—but it's not just a show. Jesus was serious about the call to the kingdom of God. He called for a response: repent and believe.

The rule of God takes place in human hearts. We come under his lordship and kingship. When we read the phrase "the kingdom of God," we could as easily read "the kingship of God" or "the rule of God." Essentially they all mean the same thing: We all come under the rule of God.

Jesus said the kingdom will come, but he revealed that the kingdom was already here. The Gospels illustrate what happens when the kingdom is present. Whenever people were in the presence of Jesus, they had a glimpse of what heaven will be like. Through the presence of Christ in our hearts, we can have the same experience. As King of the kingdom, Jesus is the portal to the new world.

IS IT WORTH THE RISK?

The congregation I led at St. Thomas' Church in Sheffield, England, for ten years was largely made up of young adults, a generation often described as Generation X. Many of them had experienced great brokenness and pain in their formative years—pain they carried through to adulthood. One of the particular things the staff at St. Thomas' noticed was that this generation of young adults was great at making friends and being friends, but it stopped there. Although there was a lot of talk about wanting to find Mr. or Miss Right, they just didn't date each other. It was as though they were paralyzed. Many people were afraid of getting hurt; they had grown up around the heartache of divorce or loveless marriages. Others just didn't have the courage to take that step of commitment that relationships require. Everybody wanted the adventure—but no one would take the risk.

Finally, it got to the point when I actually started talking about it openly. I had never before had to convince and encourage people to get together!

> **EVERYBODY WANTED THE ADVENTURE— BUT NO ONE WOULD TAKE THE RISK.**

Over the weeks and months that followed, we taught about relationships extensively. Our services provided opportunities for people to respond to issues God was bringing to the surface. Members of the staff would take young adults on mission trips and encourage them in each other's direction! I remember that on the way home from a mission trip to Nigeria, I gave up my seat so one of our guys could finally, finally, just talk to the young woman we all knew he liked!

In time we began to see people step out and take risks. People were being healed from the past and were able to move into their futures. We saw the power of a community that was not just being healed, but also becoming healthy in the way they related to each other. And the great friendships that so characterized that generation were still in place—it wasn't just about getting married. It was about wholeness, greater honesty, and transparency in relationships.

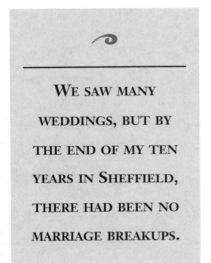

WE SAW MANY WEDDINGS, BUT BY THE END OF MY TEN YEARS IN SHEFFIELD, THERE HAD BEEN NO MARRIAGE BREAKUPS.

In the years that followed, we saw many weddings, but by the end of my ten years in Sheffield, there had been no marriage breakups. This was in a generation where one in three marriages ended in divorce and the marriage rate was falling rapidly. The kingdom of God had come and restored a community that previously had been shaped by its broken hearts.

THE TIME HAS COME

Sometimes it may feel like we are praying, "Your kingdom come," for a long time, as though the kingdom is delayed somehow. It's like those ten bridesmaids Jesus talks about in Matthew 25, waiting for the bridegroom to arrive. Five of them fall asleep, their lamps burn out, and they miss the wedding. The others are alert and prepared and so have enough oil for when the groom arrives.

Jesus says to us, "The time has come; the kingdom of God is near." Our *kairos* events bring us to the edge of a new opportunity.

So when we go through these experiences, it's as though the Lord wants each one of us to learn how to make the most of this event, so that we can enter afresh into his kingdom.

What personal *kairos* event are you currently facing? It may be a very recent event or something that has been lingering for days in your mind and heart. Do you recognize God's "nearness" in the midst of the moment? As you become more practiced in recognizing *kairos*, you will begin to notice many opportunities for God's rule and influence to come into your life in a new way, affecting your family and your work colleagues and deepening your relationship with him. Just imagine how acknowledging that the King is near can bring the wholeness we look forward to in heaven into your daily situation. Your life, your family, and your relationships could be revolutionized.

As you begin to let God into more and more of the *kairos* events of your life, you may discover that you are revisiting life lessons that have roots in some past *kairos* event—an event you

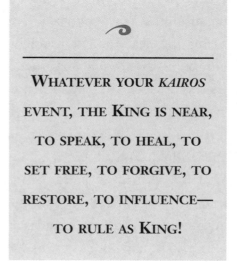

WHATEVER YOUR *KAIROS* EVENT, THE KING IS NEAR, TO SPEAK, TO HEAL, TO SET FREE, TO FORGIVE, TO RESTORE, TO INFLUENCE— TO RULE AS KING!

have yet to successfully process through the Learning Circle. What if your *kairos* event concerns pain or shame you find difficult to deal with, leaving you discouraged and depressed?[1] In the passionate life God has for you, there is more than hope—there is freedom. You have a King nearby who forgives your sin and wipes away your

---

1. Please see appendix A for more information on "The Circle and Depression."

shame, thereby bringing healing and restoration.

Whatever your *kairos* event, the King is near, to speak, to heal, to set free, to forgive, to restore, to influence—to rule as King! What we need to do is learn from Jesus how we embrace it, how we get hold of it, put our arms around all God wants to give us. Many of us probably hope that this could happen as quickly and painlessly as possible, and sometimes it might, but often the most worthwhile things in life require a little more attention and time from us, and that's not all bad!

There's no need to wait any longer. The time has come to stop gathering information about life and start living it! Jesus tells us that there are two things we need to do to make the most of our life opportunities: repent and believe. We must change our thinking in such a way that our actions are different! We can only learn from our *kairos* events and experience God's kingdom through this process of repentance and belief. Without that process, we go from event to event, crisis to crisis, never seeing a lasting change, never learning from our experiences, and repeating our mistakes. We are left feeling frustrated, bored, and disappointed.

Life is a challenge, and so is the process of learning from our *kairos* events. The call of Jesus to discipleship requires that we lay down our lives and our agendas and let God have total control of our lives. It may not be easy and we may not always like it, but in doing so, we are giving God the space to change us and do something new, to lead us in a new direction.

In the Learning Circle, we begin to see the significant events of our lives as portals into kingdom living. It is a journey of repentance and belief—a journey we can only make as we give God control of our *kairos* events and let him lead the way into a more passionate life.

CHAPTER 4

Retrace and Repent

Key Words

Repentance:
A complete change of mind and heart.
A process of transformation that takes place within a person.

Observe:
Stop, look, and listen to what actually is
happening in your kairos *moment.*

Reflect:
Ask yourselves questions about what you see
and hear—understanding is the goal!

Discuss:
Get other people's perspectives on your observations and reflections.
This is so you can be sure you are on the right track.

*H*ere you are, walking along on what you consider to be a straight path, no unexpected bends in the road, no intersections where you have to make a decision you're not prepared for. Just a nice straight walk you have taken many times before. Perhaps you have a specific purpose in mind, or perhaps you are simply walking in the general direction that seems best.

Then, seemingly out of the blue, a *kairos* moment happens and brings you to a screeching halt. You're at an intersection now, and you have to decide which way to go. You must make a choice.

You can keep on walking forward, ignoring the *kairos* moment, pretending it never happened, and hoping that the effects of it will go away.

You can stop and refuse to move in any direction at all. You may sit in regret that you ever started down this road. You don't want to be here anymore.

You can move backward, back to a familiar part of the path, a safe part of the path where you know what will happen.

Or you can pass through the portal and enter the Learning Circle. The *kairos* moment that propels you into the Circle can be positive (getting a big raise) or negative (breaking up a relationship). It can be big (the chance to start a new career) or small (an evening at home alone with your spouse). But when a *kairos* moment occurs, we must decide whether to enter the Circle. From the moment we step into the Circle, we are in a learning mode. Things will not go back to the way they were before the *kairos* event.

Jesus says we must do two things to make the most of a *kairos* opportunity: "Repent and believe the good news" (Mark 1:15). The first half of the Circle concentrates on Repent, with the three stages of Observe, Reflect, and Discuss. The second half of the Circle brings us around to Believe, with the three stages of Plan, Account, and Act. These next two chapters are an overview of the entire Circle followed by an in-depth scriptural and practical exploration of each individual step. Together we will learn how we can apply each step of the process to our lives.

Kairos is an event word. The experience has a beginning and an end. Repentance is a different sort of experience. It's a process. We do not become disciples of Jesus and stand still. Learning means continually repenting of the way we approach life, deciding to think differently. It's difficult to backtrack and review our mistakes—it's often painful. But ignoring our weaknesses and the effect they have on our lives and the lives of people we love does not make them go away. We will not progress in our walk with Jesus unless we go through the Repent side of the Circle.

> **LEARNING MEANS CONTINUALLY REPENTING OF THE WAY WE APPROACH LIFE, DECIDING TO THINK DIFFERENTLY.**

If we don't step into the Circle, we don't learn from our *kairos* events. It can be hard work to stop doing things our way and let God have total control of our lives. But when we do, we give God the space to change us and lead us in a new direction.

LESSONS FROM A SNOWBOARD

The Breen family had been in the United States for about six months. The girls had come from college in England for the holidays. It had been a hectic few months, and it was good to get some family time together. So we set off on a Breen family excursion to welcome the New Year at a friend's log cabin in Breckenridge, Colorado. Our days would be filled with skiing, with the exception of Sally, who doesn't like the combination of heights and snow. Her master plan usually calls for relaxing in the coffee shops while the rest of us seek adventure on the slopes.

The first day was a perfectly beautiful day. The sun was shining and the views were amazing. The slopes were in great shape. My children—Beccy (twenty), Libby (eighteen), and Sam (fourteen)— and I (older!) were really excited. The plan was snowboarding for Libby and Sam while Beccy and I were skiing. As the kids set off down the slope, I intended to be right behind them as soon as I was ready. As I said, things were perfect.

Perfect can change to chaos in a split second.

As Sam was making his way down the mountain, he was broadsided by another snowboarder. The force of the collision left Sam in agony, and it was immediately clear that his arm was badly injured. Libby got off her board and scrambled back up the mountain to get me and the ski patrol while Beccy stayed with Sam, offering what comfort and encouragement she could.

When we arrived at the collision site, the paramedic asked Sam lots of questions about his arm.

"On a scale of one to ten, what's your pain level?"

"Eight!"

They strapped Sam into a toboggan to pull him down to the first aid station. As the paramedic hurriedly skied downhill, she missed the moguls and fell into a ditch. Sam went flying once again.

When the paramedic recovered, she checked to see if Sam was all right.

"What's your pain level?"

"Well, it's a *ten* now!"

Once at the hospital we learned that Sam's arm was broken and had to be set in two places so that it could heal—a lot of pain and difficulty were part of that horrible process. We had a lot of *kairos* times that vacation, including some great ones, but that moment was *the kairos* event of the vacation for me.

CHANGE—PAIN OR PLEASURE?

Repentance is a vital part of our growth as disciples, but it's rarely easy. Sometimes it's because we misunderstand what it means. We often equate the act of repentance with some sort of sin or bad behavior in our lives. This probably comes from the images we have of heavy-handed preachers passing out condemnation rather than grace. But in the Bible the Greek word we translated "repent" (*metanoia*) actually means "to change one's mind." Being a disciple of Christ assumes that we will grow and change inwardly as we take on more of the character of Jesus. James 1:2–3 says, "Consider it pure joy, my brothers, whenever you face trials of many kinds, because you know that the testing of your faith develops perseverance." So, the process of repentance is not just a response to sin—it is a response to our desire to do life differently. And while it may involve pain, it leads to the pleasure of being more conformed to his character.

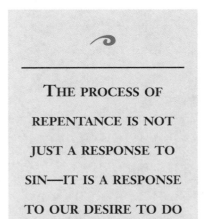

THE PROCESS OF REPENTANCE IS NOT JUST A RESPONSE TO SIN—IT IS A RESPONSE TO OUR DESIRE TO DO LIFE DIFFERENTLY.

Often we think of repentance as an outside thing, a change in our behavior, something we suddenly decide to do differently. We tell ourselves, "I'm going to give up drinking," or "I'm going to stop speeding."

Now those changes in our actions may be the result of repentance, but repentance starts within us. Jesus said, "The time has come; the kingdom of God is near." The way we enter the kingdom—to allow God to rule our lives—is to make the inner changes necessary so that the outer behavior becomes natural. Once we change on the inside, the new attitude will affect our outward actions.

I was really sad about Sam. I was back at the chalet with Sally, and she could see I was fed up about something. Normally I don't carry those things around with me. I'm not one of those people who are the grumbly bear types, but that day I was a bit cranky.

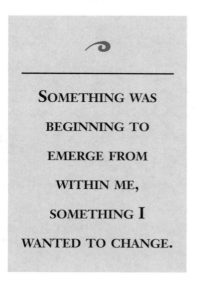

SOMETHING WAS
BEGINNING TO
EMERGE FROM
WITHIN ME,
SOMETHING I
WANTED TO CHANGE.

"What's the matter, Mike?" she asked.

"I feel responsible for Sam. I just wish I'd been there. Maybe I could have stopped the collision."

I was looking at the situation, and I wanted to change it. I wanted to change what had already happened, but of course I couldn't. Yet something was occurring in me. Something was beginning to emerge from within me, something I wanted to change.

So where does the process of repentance begin? It begins with observation.

OBSERVE

The first thing to do is to take a long honest look at the *kairos* event. If we are going to make that inner change, we need to pay attention to our thoughts, emotions, reactions, and behavior to see what might need changing.

You were listening to the country channel on the radio, and *that's* the reason why you nearly ran through a red light.

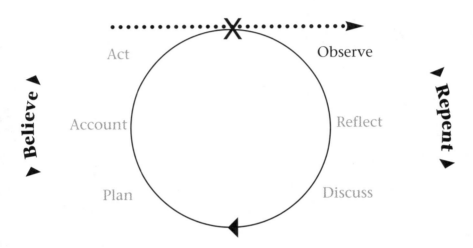

Yes, I was talking to somebody on my cell phone while I was driving so I wasn't really paying attention, and *that's* why I had a near miss on the freeway.

I remember saying that really stupid comment to my wife, and *that's* what perpetuated this entire argument.

It's just a simple observation.

Facing up to the way things are is essential if we are to change and grow into the people God wants us to be. If we take responsibility, we can see things as either a problem or a challenge to grow into what God wants us to become.

I made some simple observations when I was thinking about Sam with his broken arm. My observation was that perhaps if I had been near him, perhaps the pain he went through could have been avoided. But that was beginning to sound a bit like the father in

Finding Nemo.[1] Remember Marlin in *Finding Nemo?* He wanted to make sure that his kid never got into any places of danger. As a result, we could see that poor little Nemo was never going to learn how to do life on his own. Of course, I can't do that with Sam, but that was the beginning of my observation.

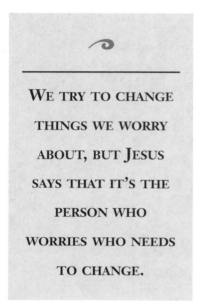

WE TRY TO CHANGE THINGS WE WORRY ABOUT, BUT JESUS SAYS THAT IT'S THE PERSON WHO WORRIES WHO NEEDS TO CHANGE.

We must be honest in our observations. We have to see things as they really are if we are to change inwardly. This is not the time to look at how others have harmed us or insist that whatever happened is someone else's fault. It's not the time to say that what we've done is not as bad as what so-and-so did or that no one was hurt, so it wasn't all that bad. If we don't make honest observations, we don't move another step around the Circle.

REFLECT

Beyond observation we have to ask questions of the observation. The normal word for that in English is "reflect." This is the next part of the process of repentance. If we are going to make that inner change, we need to look at what the event tells us. We ask questions about the *kairos* event. Why? Who? What? When? How?

"Why am I feeling this way?"

"What made me say that?

---

1. Andrew Stanton, *Finding Nemo,* DVD, directed by Andrew Stanton and Lee Unkrich (Burbank, Calif.: Buena Vista Pictures, 2003).

"When did I decide to do that?"

"How did this happen?

I looked at Sam's broken arm. It was bent and twisted. I watched it being reset. As I held his hand, I saw the tears in his eyes as the doctors tried to pop that bone back in. I wondered, *Boy, is there anything I could have done that could have made this better?*

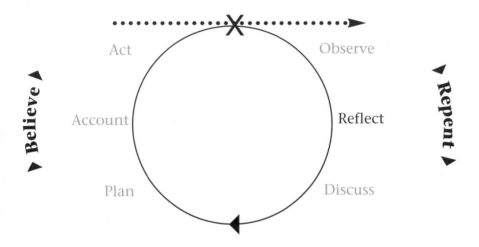

What could I have done that would have been different? Was there something I could have done that would have stopped that ·situation from happening? This is where some get stuck in the cycle of worry. We try to change things we worry about, but Jesus says that it's the person who worries who needs to change. Change happens to us when we listen to questions and begin to answer them. "Why am I worried about this when I know God is in control?"

That's repentance—when you are drawn into asking those kinds of questions. Once again our answers must be honest if real change is going to happen.

DISCUSS

Reflection should provoke conversation and discussion. The only time our observations and reflections get anywhere is when we invite others into the process. Following Jesus was never intended to be a private thing. We were never created to live in isolation; we were created to share the significant moments of our lives with other people. We need to discuss the event and our responses to it with someone else. We need to choose people who will be completely honest with us, even if the things they say are not what we want to hear. We'll talk more about *community* in the following chapters.

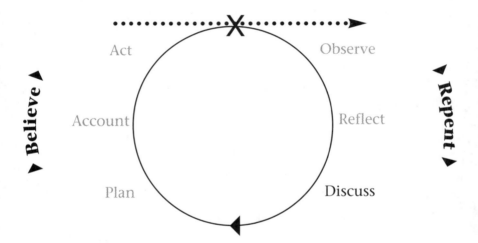

I talked to Sally. "What do you think, Sally? Was there anything I could have done? Is there anything I need to do so something like this doesn't happen again?" Somehow we have to allow the resolutions forming in our hearts to be formed into words and conversations so that there is at least one other person helping us through this process. We have a lot of excuses for skipping this part of the process—we feel inadequate to express what we are thinking.

We are afraid of what conclusions the other person will draw about us—but if we are serious about making these changes, somehow the inner changes have got to come out into the open.

Sam's accident had started a process inside of me, and I was really upset about it, yet the event was now leading toward something that

> **SOMEHOW WE HAVE TO ALLOW THE RESOLUTIONS FORMING IN OUR HEARTS TO BE FORMED INTO WORDS AND CONVERSATIONS SO THAT THERE IS AT LEAST ONE OTHER PERSON HELPING US THROUGH THIS PROCESS.**

was positive. I demonstrated my desire to make a life change by entering into the process of repentance and going through the steps of Observe, Reflect, and Discuss, but that was only half the process. To live out my desire to change, I needed to move on into the steps of faith.

CHAPTER 5

New Directions

Key Words

Believe:

- *Active trust.*
- *A trust based on something you've been persuaded about, a continuing process of belief and action.*
- *Can also be translated as faith.*
- *Something you are sure about.*

Plan:
Decide how you want the future to look now that change has begun to take effect in your life.

Account:
Be sure that others understand, support, and are able to question what you intend to do.

Act:
Go for it!

J did it again!"

How often do you say that to yourself—not with pride in an accomplishment but with frustration in making the same mistake? We smack ourselves on the forehead with disbelief at our own idiocy.

The truth is that we do not automatically learn from experience. Just living through something doesn't mean we take away anything from the experience to make things different in the future. If we did, we wouldn't repeat our mistakes as often as we do. Repentance alone will not change us. Many of us look at our lives, reflect upon them, maybe even confide in someone about a situation, but it ends there. We run out of gas before we get to the point where a lasting change can take place in the way we live of life.

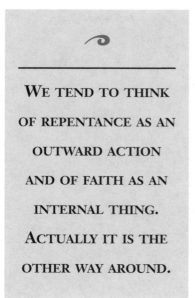

WE TEND TO THINK OF REPENTANCE AS AN OUTWARD ACTION AND OF FAITH AS AN INTERNAL THING. ACTUALLY IT IS THE OTHER WAY AROUND.

The second half of the Circle is where we begin to change our actions. The inner changes we have experienced during the first half of the Circle start to impact our outer world, our actual lives— the things we do and say.

"Believe" is another process word, like "repent." The Greek word for "believe" is *pisteuo*. It means active trust, an action based on a certainty you have now gained in your own heart. It can also be translated as "faith."

"Now faith," says the writer to the Hebrews, "is being sure of what we hope for and certain of what we do not see" (Heb. 11:1).

We often hear people say, "Well, I don't want to talk about that. Faith is a personal matter. My faith is a private thing." That's what *they* think!

Faith is an outer matter. People can see it at work in your life and at work in them through your life. Faith is an active reality. It is when you show what you are certain about through the way you live your life. Whether you talk about it or not, your faith, or lack of it, is coming through loud and clear all the time.

The New Testament is so sure about this that it tells us that if you have faith, then everyone will see it by your actions.

> What good is it, my brothers, if a man claims to have faith but has no deeds? ... Faith without deeds is dead.
>
> —James 2:14, 26

We tend to think of repentance as an outward action and of faith as an internal thing. Actually it is the other way around. Faith, by its own definition, is active; believing something and putting that belief into action are inseparable. There are three principles of faith that balance out the three principles of repentance.

PLAN

Believing is about having an intention to do something. In other words, it is having a plan. The plan should address what needs to be changed so that outward behavior can represent the change that has taken place in your heart. You've observed, reflected, and discussed. Now it's time to do something. Jesus says, *Look, you've got to have a different way of looking at your life, another way to deal with these issues. In fact, you've got to start thinking that there is another kind of plan that governs your life.*

Many *kairos* events reveal the fact that we often put something or someone in our lives in place of God. Maybe a habit has spiraled out of control and reached crisis point. As you look at and reflect on that habit, the Lord shows you a void or emptiness you try to fill with that habit. It's time for a strategy to recognize your feelings and the pressure points in your life that cause you to respond with this behavior.

After my conversation with Sally about Sam's accident, I came to the conclusion that what we needed to do was not to stop Sam from snowboarding but to invest in some wrist braces for the next time he was on the slopes. It was a simple thing we could do. We were beginning to come up with a plan.

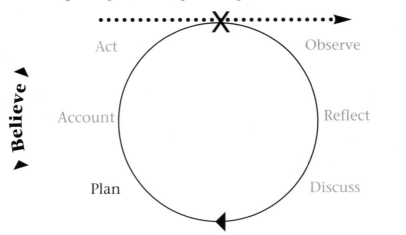

Planning is all about vision. More specifically, it's about making that vision into a reality. If you have a vision for an abundant flower garden, you read gardening books, learn about seeds and growing climates, and sketch out what you want the garden to look like. If you have a vision to do your Christmas tree in blue and silver instead of the old red and green, you hit the sales and buy some new ornaments and ribbons. We make plans and carry them out all the time. Why not plan for the vision of God's kingdom?

ACCOUNT

If a plan is going to be worth its salt, at least one other person needs to know about it to hold you accountable. The kind of change that lasts doesn't happen in private. Faith is something we're accountable for because it's something we've got to act on. Giving an account of your thoughts or failures to another person may well be difficult at first. You may feel afraid of sharing with another person or that

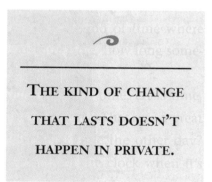

THE KIND OF CHANGE THAT LASTS DOESN'T HAPPEN IN PRIVATE.

the circumstances are too private to talk about. But these attitudes will prevent us from changing and growing as Christians.

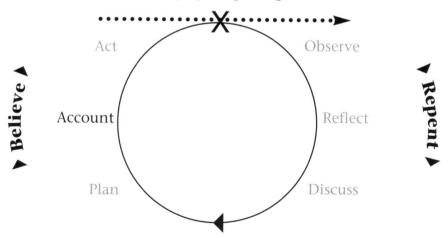

The heroes of the Bible had their mistakes written down for people around the world to see century after century, millennium after millennium. I can imagine Peter looking down from heaven at all the small groups and church services that dissect the way he denied Jesus three times. Long after his death, Peter remains an example of accountability by demonstrating how we can all learn and grow from experiencing each other's failures and successes. We also see in the New Testament that Jesus always sent his disciples out in groups of at least two. Having someone to be accountable to is part of what it means to be a disciple of Jesus.

I made a plan to buy Sam wrist braces, and I made myself accountable for it—Sally knows it, and now you're reading it in this book! If Sam breaks his wrist again, you can say to me, "Hold on, we've seen your son without a brace on his arm. Did you buy the wrist braces or not?"

We all know how easy it is to point out the mistakes or weak points in someone else. When we see how foolish someone else has been, suddenly we haven't been nearly so idiotic in our own decisions. Thinking these things may prop us up momentarily, because we think we look better in comparison. But we really don't—not to anybody else. Our relationships of accountability should never be used to shun or place guilt; they should be moments of challenge and encouragement. Hypocrites look for fault in others and are blind to their own faults. Jesus wants us to be authentic, not hypocritical.

ACT

So you have a plan and an accountability relationship. It's time to take action. Faith bubbles up within us and rises to the surface where it turns into action. Thoughts and intentions we hold within ourselves and never act on are not faith. Faith is always acted out, never kept bottled up. Take your plan off the paper and put it into your life. Go speak to that person with whom your relationship is strained. Go back to school because you believe the Lord is leading you into a new career or ministry. Join a book discussion group so you are obligated to read the books on your wish list. Send out invitations to a party for newcomers to your church. Whatever your *kairos* moment, and whatever your plan, put it into action. Plan. Account. Act. Make a plan toward change, be accountable for your plan, and put the plan into action.

Sam's arm came out of the plaster, and immediately he looked forward to an opportunity to go snowboarding again. Where we live, Phoenix, Arizona, is not known for snow, but Flagstaff is only two hours away. When we go for a day trip, Sam will have everything he needs—including his wrist braces.

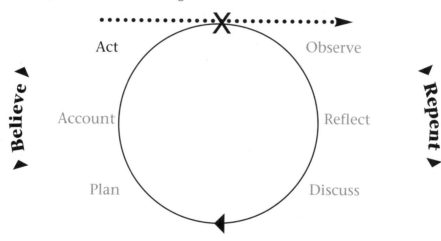

LEARNING, SLINKY STYLE

Once you become aware of the Learning Circle and put it into practice, you discover that instead of your life looking like a line that begins at salvation and ends in heaven, it looks more like a Slinky—a series of loops held together by time. Our lives are made up of events connected by time and how we respond to them. If we learn to apply the Learning Circle, we find that as we respond to each *kairos* the process of repentance and belief will lead to more of God's kingdom being revealed in our lives. Each time around the Circle means you have grown a little more and taken on a little more of the character of Christ.

Time. Kingdom. Repentance. Faith. These words are the heart of what it means to be a disciple. As if to underline the importance of discipleship, Jesus made a statement about discipleship as his last words before he went back to heaven.

> Then Jesus came to them and said, "All authority in
> heaven and on earth has been given to me.
> Therefore go and make disciples of all nations, bap-
> tizing them in the name of the Father and of the Son
> and of the Holy Spirit, and teaching them to obey
> everything I have commanded you. And surely I am
> with you always, to the very end of the age."
> —Matthew 28:18–20

The word "disciple" is sort of a religious word we don't use very much in other settings—no one would know what we're talking about. Actually it's not a religious word at all. It's simply a word that refers to somebody who chooses to learn. In Greek, it's the word *mathetes*. The word simply means "learner" or "pupil." Jesus said this: *Go out into all the world and make learners out of the people you meet. If you've become a learner, then make other people learners. If you've learned how to learn from me, then go and teach other people how to learn from me. Go and disciple them—make them learners.*

Learners of what? What is it specifically that Jesus wants us to learn? He wants us to learn how to be like him. He commands us to love others as he has loved us and that love shall serve as proof that we have *learned* from him (John 13:34–35). Throughout his ministry, Jesus teaches us how to love by teaching us what it means to be his disciple. Love is found in his example of repentance and faith (the Circle), in his daily balance of work and rest (the Semi-Circle), in his passionate relationships with everyone around him (the Triangle), in his teachings of leadership and discipleship (the Square). His love is expressed through all his ministry roles (the Pentagon), in his teaching to love and speak with the Father (the Hexagon). Our love grows as we learn to nurture our spiritual life as Jesus did (the Heptagon) and our love for others is what leads our desire to bring them to Christ (the Octagon).

When we look at the Learning Circle (and all the other *LifeShapes*), we learn to understand Jesus' words and apply them to our lives, and we are learning what it means to be a disciple because a disciple is a learner.

TRAIN TO CHANGE

My friend Walt Kallestad was talking with a friend. This man was a successful businessman but had made some significant mistakes in his personal life, and his family was about to fall apart. Walt talked at length with his friend about the difference Jesus could make to his life, his business, and his family.

"Walt, I want to change, but I can't change," he said, despondent. "I've tried to follow God before. It didn't last."

"It's not about trying," said Walt "It's about training. If you want to live as a Christian, it's not about trying to be better. You need to train to change."

How does anyone who wants to follow Jesus move forward in discipleship? The answer is surrendering to the process of change. The process of the Learning Circle will bring us back to the basics of our faith, to the cross and resurrection of Jesus. Repentance and faith reflect the cross and resurrection. Repentance is where we die to ourselves, while faith is living in Christ.

If you've chosen to learn, you've become a *mathetes*. You've become a disciple. You've allowed Jesus to enter the events of your life, however small, and teach you how to learn from them.

So that's the basic rundown, along with some great scriptural basis, for the Learning Circle. If you want to continue your study of how Jesus taught the Circle, read the Sermon on the Mount (Matt. 5–7). Every single step of the Circle can be found in that one event of Jesus' ministry. As you go through the story, see if you can find each Circle concept and how it was lived out between Jesus and his disciples. Let's move on to explore each step of the Circle in greater detail so that you may have a full understanding of how to make this a permanent part of your life.

CHAPTER 6

Stop. Look. Listen.

T wonder if this is what our father Abraham saw."

Joshua's voice wandered off into the distance, but Caleb understood exactly what Joshua was trying to say. With ten others, they had traveled from Paran up toward Canaan, through the Negev to Hebron. Caleb had heard of these places only in stories, the places where his ancestors Abraham and Isaac had walked and lived in freedom. Caleb had known only slavery; every step he took was significant. This was the homeland he had never known, the land God had promised to give his people.

It seemed that the time had come for the Israelites. With the slavery of Egypt and their miraculous deliverance behind them, they were on the threshold of their future. The Land of Promise, Canaan, was not far away now.

More importantly God had given Moses instructions:

Send some men to explore the land of Canaan, which I am giving to the Israelites. From each ancestral tribe send one of its leaders.

—Numbers 13:2

God's command to Moses was a sign reminding every Israelite tribe of the purpose of this journey. God, their deliverer, was fulfilling his promise made to Joseph and to every Israelite who had called out to God under the oppression of the Egyptians, responding to every drop of blood that had been shed, every tear that had fallen to the ground, every prayer prayed. Moses gathered twelve leaders from the tribes to undertake this reconnaissance mission.

The instructions he gave to the twelve leaders were clear and simple.

> Go up through the Negev and on into the hill country. See what the land is like and whether the people who live there are strong or weak, few or many.
> —Numbers 13:17–18

The task of the tribal leaders was to *observe*, to spend forty days looking at the Land of Promise. They had no networking to do, no places to attack; their sole purpose was simply to look—then look again and then keep looking. They would be the ones to tell their liberated people exactly what the promise of God looked like; their observations would illustrate the longings of generations. They needed to pay attention because they were the forerunners. On a practical level, their observations would guide them in developing a battle strategy. Furthermore, detailed observations of Canaan would guide the Israelites as they prepared to make a life there. They would find the most suitable areas for settlement, the agricultural qualities of the land, and the kind of produce the Israelites could expect to grow.

Moses guided the team of leaders in its observations with questions to reflect upon.

What kind of towns do they live in? Are they
unwalled or fortified? How is the soil? Is it fertile or
poor?

—Numbers 13:19–20

Back at Kadesh, the rest of the Israelite people waited. There was no telling how long this expedition would take. Would the twelve explorers even make it back?

They did make it back. The Israelite community gathered with Moses and Aaron to hear a report of the exploration. All of the explorers agreed that the land they had explored was amazing. The agricultural potential was astounding. The people could live very comfortably in the land.

As the discussions continued, ten of the leaders began to express doubts about whether the Israelites could ever defeat the people living in the land:

But the people who live there are powerful, and the
cities are fortified and very large.

—Numbers 13:28

This was more than Caleb could take. The representative of the tribe of Judah had a different perspective to share. As he journeyed those forty days, his sense of certainty about God's promise had not waned. If anything, he was more certain than ever. After all, it was *God* who had sent them to look at Canaan, because he wanted to give it to them. The God who defeated the Egyptians would defeat the inhabitants of Canaan. Caleb's plan was simple:

We should go up and take possession of the land, for
we can certainly do it.

—Numbers 13:30

Caleb had little support. With the exception of Joshua, the other tribal leaders continued to spread a negative report among the tribes of Israel—each revelation added to the drama:

"The land we looked at devours those who live in it."

"They will eat us alive."

"The people there are huge, like giants!"

"We felt like grasshoppers next to them. And worse, when they looked at us, they looked down on us like we were grasshoppers."

It was all too much for Israel. Although they were physically free, their hearts and minds were still held captive by fear and doubt. As far as they were concerned, they had been oppressed and enslaved for generations, and they always would be. Soon they turned on their leaders. Moses and Aaron had gotten them into one fine mess by bringing them from Egypt only to be killed by Canaanites. They needed someone who would lead them back to Egypt. Back home. Back to where they knew what life held for them.

Joshua and Caleb were at the limit of their patience. They knew the obstacles, but they also saw that the Israelites were about to throw away God's promise and choose to be enslaved. They tried to call the people to account, to challenge them about the decision they were making. It wasn't just Moses and Aaron they were rebelling against. It was God! Their deliverer! Did they not understand?

> Only do not rebel against the LORD. And do not be afraid of the people of the land, because we will swallow them up. Their protection is gone, but the LORD is with us.
>
> —Numbers 14:9

The people didn't listen. Instead they prepared to stone Joshua and Caleb to death. As for the Promised Land, they were not going anywhere. Then the glory of the Lord appeared at the Tent of Meeting for every Israelite to see, ready to respond. God was losing patience as well. It was time to sit up and pay attention.

MORE THAN LOOKING

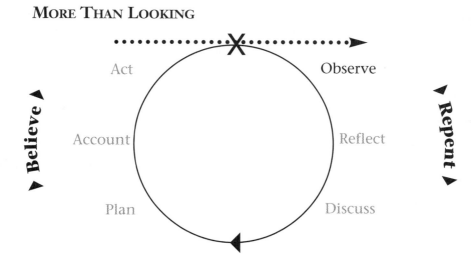

Observation is more than just looking. As Joshua and Caleb show us, observation is a fact-finding mission that leads to great discoveries. It's easy to look at a situation, to see something and not actually observe what is happening at all. Observation is not a practice limited to our eyes. It involves all our senses. We remember the smell of a place, the taste of a favorite meal, what it was like to touch something. We recall what we heard in conversation. When we observe our *kairos*, we must take note of everything that is happening around us and within us.

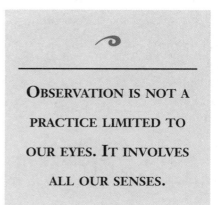

OBSERVATION IS NOT A PRACTICE LIMITED TO OUR EYES. IT INVOLVES ALL OUR SENSES.

When we look at something closely, it helps us to see what is happening on the surface and beneath it. The Greek language of the New Testament has several words we might translate as "look" or "see." One thing they have in common is a nuance that expresses how seeing goes beyond simply looking at things on a casual level. Seeing means perceiving, discerning, considering, contemplating.

Observation was central to Jesus' life and ministry. Jesus traveled to Jerusalem to celebrate a feast. He arrived at a place called Bethesda. Bethesda had a pool surrounded by five porches. But it was no ordinary pool. Occasionally an angel would visit and stir the waters. The first person who got into the pool after the water was stirred would be healed. As a result, Bethesda was overcrowded with people who were watching and waiting, desperate to be healed of their sicknesses.

Jesus was also watching, but he wasn't watching the pool. He saw a man who had been an invalid for thirty-eight years. When Jesus asked the man if he wanted to get well, the man responded by saying there was no one to help him into the pool when the waters were stirred. But Jesus didn't have the pool in mind. Telling the man to get up and walk, he healed him completely.

It was a wonderful miracle, but the religious leaders, suffering from their own form of blindness, were angry that Jesus has healed a man on the Sabbath.

Jesus' response is quite simple.

> I tell you the truth, the Son can do nothing by him-
> self; he can do only what he sees his Father doing,
> because whatever the Father does the Son also does.
> —John 5:19

Jesus explained to the religious leaders: *You don't get it. I'm not acting independently. I'm walking around, watching. But I am looking at what my Father is doing. And when he shows me what he is doing, then I simply respond.*

Jesus took his lead from his Father in heaven. He paid close attention to the world around him to see where his Father was working, how he wanted to move, what he wanted said. Observation gives us a perspective—God's perspective—that we wouldn't have otherwise. Jesus watched what his Father was doing so he would know what he was to do and he encourages his disciples to do the same.

When Jesus spoke to a Samaritan woman at the well, her life was changed forever. Soon her community would hear about Jesus and discover him for itself. However, when the disciples saw Jesus talking to her, they couldn't see past the fact that Jews and Samaritans didn't mix. None of them said a word, but surely their facial expressions said it all. Why was Jesus talking to a woman? Wasn't she a Samaritan? What did she want, anyway? The Samaritan woman must have gotten the hint. After coming out at the hottest part of day to get some water, she went home without her water jar!

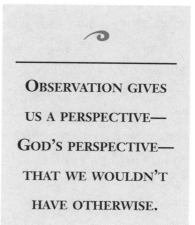

OBSERVATION GIVES US A PERSPECTIVE—GOD'S PERSPECTIVE—THAT WE WOULDN'T HAVE OTHERWISE.

Because the disciples were looking at things just on the surface, they missed the opportunity to learn what God was doing. They saw the Samaritan, and they saw a woman. But they didn't see the potential in the situation, and they didn't see how God was moving in her life—how open she was to the Gospel.

When she left, they just got on with business, asking Jesus if he wanted some food. But Jesus wasn't going to let them miss this; there was something they needed to learn. They needed to learn how to see what was really going on in that situation.

> Do you not say, "Four months more and then the
> harvest"? I tell you, open your eyes and look at the
> fields! They are ripe for harvest.
> —John 4:35

In other words, *Guys, you're missing this! And you can't see because you're not observing. You see a Samaritan woman. You see that it's dinnertime. But do you know what is happening here, what is really happening? The kingdom of God is near. She is just one of many people who are so hungry that they are ripe to hear the good news. Look at the people around here. It's harvest time!*

If the disciples looked carefully, really observed, then they would discover something amazing. They would discover that God was on the move and they had the opportunity to get involved. If only they would see it.

TAKE A CHANCE

When your negative bank balance becomes a terrifying *kairos* moment, looking at the birds of the air has not really helped one bit! Maybe you have learned to recognize your *kairos* moment, but you don't know how to make observations that will help you in the process of actually learning from your experiences. How do we, as lifelong learners, develop our skills of observation as we go through the process of repentance?

Some of us may find this stage of the Circle easier than others; to some it may come naturally. The good news is that like those first disciples, we can learn from Jesus. God is good to us; each stage of the Learning Circle is a skill we can put into practice and learn from.

When I first arrived at the Community Church of Joy in Phoenix, I sensed one group God specifically wanted us to reach out to was the young families in the community. During our Saturday night service, which I was responsible for, I looked at some of the young families with their children. I wondered how we could serve them better, how we could be a blessing to the children, but also to their parents. I met people who were struggling with the pressures of raising children while holding down full-time jobs. They had so many plates spinning in the air at the same time, I wasn't sure how they kept everything going.

I looked around our church campus. We had a preschool and school that gathered literally hundreds of children from the local community. Some were members of the church family—many weren't. How could we serve and reach this generation of young families? I wanted to find ways of encouraging and affirming family life. I wanted to tell people that it was great that they wanted to spend time with their kids. I also wanted to encourage people to make time for their marriages. We started having meals together and playing volleyball after the service. It was a great start as we began to build relationships. People of all ages began to hang out together. But there was something else. I just wasn't sure what it was.

A few months later, some friends and I went to a Christian event on the other side of the city. As church buildings go, this church was absolutely stunning. The children's venue was built around the theme of a castle, and it even had a drawbridge and a moat! It was so cool it made me want to be a kid again. The lobby had a fantastic café and bookshop. The classrooms, the sanctuary, everything about it just about took your breath away. It was a great church with great space. Just before the event began, I made a visit to the bathroom. Again, it was as perfect as a restroom could be! On the back of the door I saw an advertisement. A couple having a romantic, candlelit meal looked lovingly at one another. Underneath were the words "Date Night."

Part of the ministry of the church involved providing the local community with the opportunity for children to spend time in activities at the church so that parents could go out on a date. What a terrific idea!

The event was great. As we left, we talked about what a wonderful time we had and how amazing the venue was. But I just couldn't get the image of the Date Night advertisement out of my mind. Of all the things we had seen and experienced that night, the poster on the back of the bathroom door had most arrested my attention! A few days later I mentioned it to my team, saying what a great idea it was. A few days later, I mentioned it again. And again! The picture would not leave me alone, and I couldn't drop it. I realized that the Lord had captured my attention through this image. Over time it became apparent that this was what God wanted us to do. This was our next step as part of our mission to serve our church family and the local community.

OF ALL THE THINGS WE HAD SEEN AND EXPERIENCED THAT NIGHT, THE POSTER ON THE BACK OF THE BATHROOM DOOR HAD MOST ARRESTED MY ATTENTION!

Stop, Look, and Listen

When children learn to cross the road, they learn three key words:

Stop.

Look.

Listen.

Sometimes we miss out on observation because we do not take the time to stop when a *kairos* event happens. Perhaps we are under a lot of pressure because of a specific situation. After all, what does someone who has just lost a job need to look at? Surely we just need to get out there and get another job so we can provide for our families. We feel we just have to do something, so we start asking questions straight away, or we make plans or act on decisions we make.

But what if we haven't got the full picture? It's easy to make assumptions when you are in the middle of your *kairos*. Careful observation slows you down long enough for you to engage—to look and to listen.

It was a cold, gray Thursday in Sheffield, England. Mark was enjoying an unexpected break between patients at his dental office. One of his dental nurses, Sarah, opened the door to his office.

"There's a man outside and he says he needs to see you."

Mark sighed. *There goes my fifteen minutes off!*

An older man walked in and sat in the dental chair. After the usual polite exchange between patient and dentist, Mark looked at his patient's teeth. There didn't seem to be anything wrong with them. After the checkup, the patient apologized for how he was dressed.

"I've been working in my garden, you see."

Up until then Mark hadn't been paying much attention to the

patient's fashion. His clothes were torn and shabby, like garden clothes. But it was November. No one worked in the garden at that time of year. Mark realized that his patient was embarrassed about his appearance and so had offered a "gentleman's excuse." It wasn't long before the checkup was over and the patient left.

About ten minutes later, Sarah knocked on the door of the office.

"Mark, can we speak to you for a minute?"

Mark went outside to the reception desk, where he found two angry dental nurses and an even angrier receptionist.

"That patient was really rude to me! He complained about the cost of his treatment! But he already owes us fifty dollars that he has not paid from the last time he was here!"

"He's trying to take us for a ride! We need to do something about him!"

"We should cross him off our books and tell him he can't come back!"

As Mark listened to his staff's complaints, he pictured his patient. He was quite a defensive character, clearly embarrassed about how he looked. This was a man who clearly wasn't in a position to pay off what he owed.

Mark's observations made him wonder whether God wanted him to try a different response to the situation. What was God doing here? Why was this man so embarrassed, so aggressive?

In the end Mark decided to write off the debt completely. He noted in all the financial records that the patient was debt free. He explained to his staff that they were going to apply different principles in this circumstance. They were going to forgive and let it go. The staff was surprised, but Mark was in charge, so they went along with it.

In the months that followed, Mark heard from other dental practices that this patient was in the habit of running up debts and making complaints. Every other dental practice had pursued the money it was owed. In turn, the patient had made a complaint to the local health authority and filed a lawsuit against each practice. Even though his claims were unfounded, the health authority was obliged to investigate, causing months of inconvenience for the practices involved. But Mark had let it go, so the patient had left his practice alone.

Mark realized that paying attention to the situation had helped him share kingdom principles with his staff. Furthermore, it had saved him from wasting a lot of time and money dealing with a pointless lawsuit.

THE INDUCTIVE METHOD

Meet Sir Francis Bacon, an English philosopher, scientist, and author who lived from 1561 to 1626. He is credited as being the first person to explain induction. The inductive method begins with observation. From these observations, one draws a tentative conclusion. Then instead of trying to make everything else fit the conclusion, the conclusion becomes the source of further experiments to test the validity and range of application of each conclusion. This leads to further tentative conclusions that are likewise tested. Thus the process of scientific induction proceeds indefinitely.

When we use the inductive method, we gather specific information as we look at something in detail. Then we use our own knowledge and experience to make an observation about what must be true. As disciples of Jesus, we don't stop at our own knowledge. We are learners; so we pray, we look at the life of Jesus, and we look at the Word of God to help us as we observe. We use a series of observations to come to our conclusions.

Induction often starts with looking at the big picture with the observations that follow possibly becoming more and more detailed as you test out your conclusions. For example, you may look at society today and feel, broadly speaking, that we have become increasingly permissive about our moral values. It's a general observation.

But that observation may become confirmed as things get more specific. You turn on the TV at prime time to watch a show with your family, and you see things and hear language you are not comfortable seeing yourself, let alone allowing your children to see. You started with an overall general observation, but everywhere you turn, the smaller observations of life seem to confirm it.

If we are going to learn from the experiences of life, then we need to see what is happening. We need to watch our attitudes, our reactions, and our overreactions. We need to observe how we behave in relationships, the way we speak and conduct ourselves. When something about a situation stays in your mind, perhaps it's a nudge to pay particular attention. Look again. And again. When something catches your eye, it's worth another look. Rather than leaving our observations behind, we need to attend to them.

In the Learning Circle, our observations help us do what Jesus did—ask the question, "What is God doing?"

When we have carefully observed our *kairos* event and gathered as much information as we can (these things get easier with practice!), then we are ready for the next stage of repentance: Reflect.

CHAPTER 7

What Does It Mean?

~⟋⟍◗

This day I defy the ranks of Israel! Give me a man
and let us fight each other.

—1 Samuel 17:10

*K*ing Saul and his army were terrified.

Goliath's challenge sent shivers down the spine of every
Israelite warrior. Goliath was the nine-foot-tall Philistine champion
from Gath. His armor weighed in at 125 pounds. The point on his
spear alone weighed fifteen pounds. And now this giant was asking
for a fight. But he didn't want to fight army against army. He
wanted to fight just one Israelite man to settle the dispute between
the Philistines and Israelites once and for all.

With Goliath on the side of the Philistines, they already had an
unfair advantage, but this proposal was ridiculous. One Israelite
man against that giant? It was like choosing to walk to your death.
It wasn't a fight; it was an invitation to the slaughter!

For forty days, in the morning and evening, Goliath taunted
the Israelite army. Every day the Israelites became more demoral-
ized. As far as they were concerned, they didn't stand a chance. No

one volunteered to cross the valley between the Israelite and Philistine armies.

Jesse was an old man, too old to serve in Saul's army. But he had three sons who had joined up. Jesse wanted to know how his sons were doing, how the battle was going. His youngest son, David, looked after Jesse's sheep. He was old enough to go on his own to find out how his brothers were getting along. So Jesse sent David on his way to get some information.

Early the next morning, David set off for the camp. When he arrived, the Israelite army was moving into its battle positions, shouting war cries. The Philistines moved to face the Israelites, ready to fight.

The tension was incredible. David had to have a closer look. He left the food with the keeper of the supplies and ran out to the battle lines to talk to his brothers. While they were talking, the brothers were interrupted by a loud, deep, angry voice.

"Let's settle this fight once and for all! You call yourself warriors? No, you are boys! No, you're a group of women! Israel has no army! I'm laying down the challenge again. Are any of you strong enough, man enough to take me on? Come on, Israel, send me a man and we will settle this fight once and for all!"

David looked to where the sound was coming from. There he saw the biggest human "thing" he had every seen. And he was laughing at the Israelite army!

Goliath hadn't finished speaking, but the Israelites weren't sticking around to hear the rest. David was dragged along with all the warriors who were running for their lives.

David could see the fear on the soldiers' faces. They were more than scared; they were petrified. Back at the camp there were all sorts of conversations among the soldiers.

"Have you ever seen anything like this? Every day he challenges us, puts us down."

"When you are nine feet tall, you kind of have the upper hand."

"But have you heard the latest? The king has offered a massive reward for whoever takes out Goliath. The soldier gets to marry the king's daughter, gets lots of money, and his family will never pay taxes again!"

"Yes, but the soldier has to kill the giant to get it, and that is never going to happen."

David watched and listened, listened and watched. Not knowing of the king's reward, David thought something didn't quite add up. So he spoke up: "What will be done for the man who kills this Philistine and removes this disgrace from Israel?" (1 Sam. 17:26).

> **WHILE EVERYONE ELSE WAS PANICKING ABOUT THE SIZE OF THE PROBLEM, DAVID WAS LOOKING AT THE SIZE OF THE TARGET!**

The soldiers stopped talking to work out where the question had come from. They looked around and discovered a teenager who looked like he wanted an answer to his question. Was he serious? "Who is this uncircumcised Philistine that he should defy the armies of the living God?" David asked.

It seemed a rather inappropriate question. Among all the Israelites present, nobody cared about who this monster was. All they cared about was how not to get killed by him.

But David was looking at the situation and asking important questions. Even under the surface of that reflection about "the uncircumcised Philistine" was a major point that would determine David's next move.

David challenged the Israelites: "Why is no one going out there to kill him? What's the big problem? He's just a big target. What are

we waiting for? Has everybody forgotten something really important about this whole thing? The giant isn't even circumcised. That
means he's not protected by the Lord Almighty! We Israelites bear
the symbol of a covenant with the living God. That means our
enemy is his enemy, our battle is his battle. They may have Goliath,
but God's on our side. The living God will fight for us and he will
totally win. Goliath may look like a giant to us, but he's not even
an ant to God. So, come on, let's take him!"

David understood something the people around him didn't, so
the discussions that followed didn't go well. While everyone else
was panicking about the size of the problem, David was looking at
the size of the target!

"What are you doing here?" said David's oldest brother, Eliab.
He didn't rate his youngest brother too highly and was furious
when he saw him asking the kind of questions he himself couldn't
ask. "And what about that tiny flock of little sheep you are supposed to be looking after?" Eliab sneered at David. "You think I
don't know you? You're only here to get a seat to watch the fight!
Why don't you just run along home, David; look after the little
sheep and leave us to do the job around here."

"What's your problem?" asked David "What have I done now?"

David was even more determined, so he walked away and talked
to other soldiers. It was not long before his comments reached the
ears of King Saul, and David was summoned to meet him.

By the time David reached the king, it was all settled in his
mind. He's got a plan: "Let no one lose heart on account of this
Philistine; your servant will go and fight him" (1 Sam. 17:32).

King Saul doesn't get it either. "But you're only a kid. This guy
has been eating people like you for breakfast since *he* was a kid!"

So David gave an account to the king about why he wanted to
take on Goliath. He told Saul about all the victories God had given

him in the past as shepherd of his flock. The way David saw it, the God who protected him from the lion and the bear in the past would deal with Goliath. When Saul tried to give David his kingly armor, again David explained why he couldn't use Saul's armor to win this fight. As far as David was concerned, this was God's battle. What use was Saul's armor? Besides, it was huge and heavy, not like David at all.

David went to battle.

When he first saw David, Goliath was surprised and entertained. Nevertheless he intended to squash the little squirt.

But David was ready: "I hope everybody's watching. Because today everyone around here is going to see that it doesn't matter how big you are. God doesn't need weapons to save his people. This is God's battle, Goliath, and that means you are going to die now!"

He ran toward Goliath and, with five stones and a sling, quickly coming up against the greatest giant-sized killer Israel had ever known. One stone smack in the middle of Goliath's forehead took care of Israel's problem. Imagine the thud when Goliath hit the ground face-first.

God had a covenant relationship with Israel that had been in existence since the days of Abraham. But that day on the battlefield, David was the only one who actually reflected upon and asked questions about what that meant. The battle

IF OBSERVATION BRUSHES AWAY THE DUST THAT COVERS THE SURFACE OF OUR *KAIROS*, THEN REFLECTION IS A DRILL THAT PENETRATES THE ROCK TO REVEAL WHERE THE GOLD CAN BE FOUND.

was a *kairos* moment. The questions David asked helped pave the way for the kingdom of God to be extended through the situation. The same is true for us. When we go through our *kairos* times, our observations need to be closely followed by reflection. If observation brushes away the dust that covers the surface of our *kairos,* then reflection is a drill that penetrates the rock to reveal where the gold can be found.

BEYOND OBSERVATION

Perhaps your *kairos* at work involved a tense conversation with a work colleague. You observed something in your coworker's body language that told you that something wasn't quite right. The tone of voice was sharper than usual; the person wouldn't maintain eye contact with you. Careful observation tells you that *something* is going on, but you are not sure what it is. Observation can be intuitive, but it doesn't always lead directly to the facts of a situation. This is where reflection comes in.

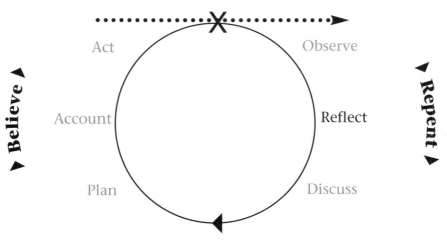

The process of reflection goes deeper than observation, providing more concrete information than what you gain simply by intuition. Reflection gives you the time you need to think through all of the information you have received from your observation.

For some of us, most likely introverts, reflection happens internally. You keep thinking over your *kairos* and your observations, chewing them over, thinking on each detail, asking questions. As you reflect on that conversation with your work colleague, you think, *I wonder how Greg is doing. He said the other day that he'd been to the doctor for tests. I wonder if he got the results. He's been under a lot of pressure at work recently and has been working long hours, even weekends sometimes. I wonder how his family is doing. I wonder if there is anything I can do to help.*

If you didn't take the time to think it over, then you might assume from your observation that Greg is in a foul mood and should be avoided at all costs! Your reflections tell you some concrete things about Greg. Instead of getting angry with Greg and walking away, you make yourself available for God to use you in that situation. It could be a kingdom opportunity, a chance for God to break through into the present and give you the power to do incredible things on his behalf.

Maybe like David in the story earlier, your reflections may be more external. He processed his thoughts out loud. Yes, Goliath was big, ugly, and intimidating. But he was also uncircumcised. This meant that God didn't look after him the way he looked after the Israelites. This meant that an Israelite victory wasn't a vague hope or dream; it was a certainty.

THE QUESTION HABIT

A simple way to reflect is to ask questions of what you see, of the situation you experience. If it helps, write your observations and reflections down on a piece of paper.

You've had an argument with your spouse, but what makes it such a *kairos* is that it's *the* argument you always have. It's like you never seem to resolve this one. Your observation is that you're both angry, and that you just walked out of the room because you weren't going to listen anymore. But why? What reflections can you make about how you spoke, how you argued, why you walked away, why you feel the way you do? As we go further into our reflections, asking questions and pondering over the answers, we can begin to identify what God may be trying to say to us.

> **AS WE GO FURTHER INTO OUR REFLECTIONS, ASKING QUESTIONS AND PONDERING OVER THE ANSWERS, WE CAN BEGIN TO IDENTIFY WHAT GOD MAY BE TRYING TO SAY TO US.**

Reflection is a common model of teaching in both the Old and New Testaments. In the Old Testament, we see it in the wisdom books. Job, Psalms, Proverbs, Ecclesiastes, and the Song of Songs have wide and varied themes. Some portions are written as songs, others as poetry. What they have in common is that they reflect upon human experiences in order to help solve and understand the problems of life. These are more than self-help books. In the midst of their reflections, the authors search to find God and how he works. These writers see reflection as a tool for receiving God's help.

> How can a young man keep his way pure?
> By living according to your word.
> —Psalm 119:9

> The proverbs of Solomon son of David, king of Israel:
> for attaining wisdom and discipline;
> for understanding words of insight; ...
>
> —Proverbs 1:1–2

As we reflect on all this, we may conclude that the righteous and the wise are in God's hands, but no person knows whether love or hate awaits him or her (Eccl. 9:1). These wisdom books invite us to learn by reflecting on our experiences and upon God.

Jesus stepped out of the boat to meet a crowd that was excited and expectant. He had just returned from the country of the Gerasenes. While he was there he had met a man who was overwhelmed by demons. Jesus set the man free from the demons who had ruined his life, but the people of the town were so frightened by the power of what they had seen that they begged Jesus to leave them.

Now Jairus, one of the local religious leaders, fell at Jesus' feet. His daughter was dying and Jairus was desperate. As Jesus walked toward Jairus' home, the crowd followed, pushing for a view of what would happen next. A woman in the crowd had been hemorrhaging for twelve years. She spent all her money on doctors, but nothing worked. Desperate, she pushed her way through the crowd. *If I can just reach him,* she probably thought. *He doesn't have to say anything. But maybe if I just touch his clothing, maybe that way I'll get healed.* Eventually, the woman saw an opportunity. She reached out and touched the edge of his cloak. She was healed instantly and completely.

Jesus stopped walking without putting on his brake lights, and the crowd nearly fell over each other.

"Who touched me?"

Jesus was surrounded by people. But nobody came forward.

"It could have been anyone," said Peter "Look how many people there are! Everyone is crowding around you." This wasn't the first time Jesus had walked among a crowd. What was the big deal?

But Jesus said, "Someone definitely touched me. I felt power go out from me."

When the woman realized she couldn't hide anymore, she told Jesus everything. He commended her and sent her on her way.

When Jesus asked, "Who touched me?" he reflected on his experience. He took hold of his observations and searched for an answer. When that woman grabbed his cloak, it was about more than being part of the jostling crowd. It was a kingdom opportunity.

Some of the letters of the New Testament carry on with the idea of reflection in discipleship by encouraging the readers, then and now, to reflect upon their lives. As Paul discipled Timothy, he encouraged him to reflect upon his observations of life and to look to God for insight into how he can apply them to his situation.

> No one serving as a soldier gets involved in civilian
> affairs—he wants to please his commanding officer.
> Similarly, if anyone competes as an athlete, he does
> not receive the victor's crown unless he competes
> according to the rules. The hardworking farmer
> should be the first to receive a share of the crops.
> Reflect on what I am saying, for the Lord will give
> you insight into all this.
>
> —2 Timothy 2:4–7

When James wrote to the members of a Christian community, he also led it in asking questions to get it to understand more about itself and its relationship with God.

> What causes fights and quarrels among you? Don't
> they come from your desires that battle within you?

> You want something but don't get it. You kill and
> covet, but you cannot have what you want. You
> quarrel and fight. You do not have, because you do
> not ask God. When you ask, you do not receive,
> because you ask with wrong motives, that you may
> spend what you get on your pleasures.
>
> —James 4:1–3

As disciples of Jesus in today's world, we can learn a great deal by applying this biblical principle of reflection to our lives. Reflection is essential in the journey through the repentance stage of the Learning Circle. When we reflect we have an opportunity to ask why a situation happened, why we are feeling certain emotions. But when we start asking questions, we need to be completely honest with our answers. Honesty lies at the heart of repentance and is key when it comes to lasting change.

We also need to spend time reading the Bible and take time out to pray so that Jesus is our guide for this stage of the process. Without continually inviting Jesus to lead us through this process, it's easy to see things merely from our human perspective and miss out on God's kingdom. It's always good to work out why we do the things we do, but we want more than self-help. Remember, the biblical process of reflection leads us to learn more from Jesus. The Bible turns the light on areas and attitudes of our lives that may be in the dark. Spending time with God in

IT'S ALWAYS GOOD TO WORK OUT WHY WE DO THE THINGS WE DO, BUT WE WANT MORE THAN SELF-HELP.

prayer will give a greater understanding of what is happening in our lives.

It's possible that introverts who enjoy time spent alone will find this stage of the Learning Circle a lot easier than the extroverts among us. But it's still important for all of us!

EVERYDAY REFLECTION

We can introduce reflection into every part of our lives.

What questions do you need to ask of the *kairos* events you are currently experiencing?

It could be any of these: Who? What? When? Where? How? Why?

For some of us, reflection doesn't come naturally. If that is the case, we may have to put in some time to learn to reflect on what is going on in life.

Mal and Chriscelle were keen to apply all aspects of the Circle to every part of their lives. But like all of us, they were busy! So they began to find ways to take the time to reflect. Here's how Mal describes their experience of the Circle:

> Three times a year my wife and I aim to have a "Love" weekend. This is to retreat, have fun and spend quality time together, get a break from the normal pressures of life, and to be intentional in reviewing and planning from the *kairos* moments of our lives. If we are ahead of the game, this is a well-planned weekend full of good food, a great location, and maybe taking in a show or movie. In a hectic season, we may begin to sense an urgent need to catch up on our lives and understand what areas God may be at work in. So, we take an afternoon to retreat and catch up.

When we go away we normally take a flipchart, paper, and pens. We know the six stages of the Circle well, but we still draw a Circle as a visual reminder. Then we focus on identifying the "defining events" of the recent months. Over time we have found these defining events fall into seven main categories, so we now purposefully take an inventory of each of those areas to make sure we aren't missing where God is trying to get our attention. Only after we've identified the events in each area of our life do we start to take them, one by one, through the process of the Circle. Taking an inventory of the events only takes a few minutes; but taking those events around the Circle, with time for reflection, discussion, prayer, and planning for each, can take much more than a weekend!

The seven areas are:

1. God. How are we doing with God? Individually? Together? What could be better? Where do we sense his hand and voice at work? Where are we being challenged?

2. Relationships. How are we as a family? Is everybody happy? Are we, as parents, getting individual time with each of the children? How are our extended family relationships? And our friends (our God family)? Who is God bringing to our attention in this season, and how do we need to respond?

3. Time. How is our current timetable structure, and how is the rhythm of our days, weeks, and months? What's on the calendar? Do we have planned vacation and retreat time? When do we have visitors? Do we have enough rest time and space to be reactive to the unforeseen?

4. Money. What are our account balances? Income, expenses, and monthly cash flow? Are we being challenged to give or tithe more or in a different way? Where do we need to be better stewards?

5. Home. Is our house working? Where do we need to respond? What plans do we have? What's the priority to do next? What other stuff do we need to take care of—cars, for instance?

6. Work. How's it going? What are the main issues? Is the role clear? What are the people situations—teams, support, People of Peace? Does child care work?

7. Church. How's it going? Are we investing in our main areas of vision and calling? Where do we need to respond?

If your primary focus of work is church (as it is in our case), you might be tempted to combine those last two categories. We have found it healthy to make the distinction between "doing life" in a church community and reviewing a paid role that has a job description (however inaccurate that might be—that might be the *kairos*!). This also allows for seasons of one partner not being in a church role and any other entrepreneurial schemes you may have on the side.

Some of these questions are more relevant to a particular season of life, especially considering issues of children at different life stages. We may not nail every issue right away; sometimes we need to take more time for reflection and observation before we can even begin to look at what putting our faith into action means on that issue. At times our periods of reflection involve waiting, prayer, confusion, and even mistakes. At other times, we sense the conviction of the Holy Spirit about an area where we need to change. Some of the areas we review are quick and easy; some are laborious and time consuming.

Perhaps you are not in a position to take three weekends a year to review. You still need to reflect. You can adapt the ideas and apply the principles to your life. Perhaps on the drive to work or as you do the grocery shopping, you can take a few moments to reflect upon what is happening in your life and ask Jesus to show you what he wants to do.

Reflection can be revealing. Sometimes it can be a humbling experience as we realize who we are

IT WOULD BE SO EASY TO KEEP OUR THOUGHTS TO OURSELVES AND CARRY ON. BUT THIS IS NOT REPENTANCE AS JESUS TEACHES.

or why we behave the way we do. But that still does not complete the process of repentance. It would be so easy to keep our thoughts to ourselves and carry on. But this is not repentance as Jesus teaches. If we are serious about change, then we need to embrace the stage where we share what we are learning with others. It's time to talk about what's really going on. Discuss.

CHAPTER 8

Let's Talk

*T*hey had to go.

Saul was a Jew from Tarsus. He had been educated in Jerusalem under Gamaliel, the president of the Sanhedrin, the "Supreme Court" of the Jewish people. As a Pharisee, Saul was totally committed to following the Jewish laws and customs that demand unwavering obedience. Yet there was one group he opposed more than any other. In fact, he despised them. They were followers of Jesus. He had them thrown into prison, whipped, and beaten in synagogues. He even approved of their murder.

But persecuting the followers of Jesus in Jerusalem was not enough for Saul. All of them had to be eliminated, and he was prepared to track down every one of them. He contacted other Jewish leaders in Damascus who invited him to Damascus to drag the Christians in chains back to Jerusalem. They had to go.

It was about noon, and Saul had nearly reached Damascus. Suddenly he saw a bright light. It was so overpowering that he fell to the ground. He heard a voice:

Saul, Saul, why do you persecute me?

—Acts 9:4

Bewildered, Saul's heart and mind raced. What was going on? Who was this? It had all happened so quickly, there was no time to work out what was going on. And now this voice. Saul couldn't make out who it was. But the man knew Saul and knew exactly what he was about to do. Saul didn't recognize him but knew he was incredibly powerful. All he could do was ask, "Who are you? Who are you, Lord?"

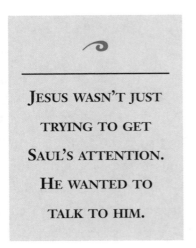

JESUS WASN'T JUST TRYING TO GET SAUL'S ATTENTION. HE WANTED TO TALK TO HIM.

Jesus wasn't just trying to get Saul's attention. He wanted to talk to him. The conversation would define the rest of Saul's life. *Saul, Saul, why do you persecute me? It is hard for you to kick against the goads. When you attack these people, it's me you are attacking. It's me you are trying to crush. You can't resist me. You're like an ox trying to kick against his master's goading stick, only to hurt yourself more in the process. Your conscience is eating at you, and the more it gets to you, the more violent you become. But it's you who gets hurt the most. You cannot ignore it anymore. You cannot ignore me anymore.*

Saul's original plans clearly had to change.

I have a plan for you, Saul. I've come to talk to you because from now on you will serve me and be my witness. You will tell people that I am real and that I'm alive. And I have a special task for you. I want you to go to the Gentiles to open their eyes, so that they too can know me.

"What do I do now, Lord?"

Get up and go to Damascus. Someone will meet you there and tell you the next step.

The light was so bright that Saul was blinded. Used to being an in-charge kind of guy, Saul now had to depend on others and be led to Damascus by his fellow travelers. He couldn't see a thing for three days. Then God sent a believer called Ananias to the house where Saul was staying. He prayed for Saul to receive his sight and to be filled with the Holy Spirit. He was also the first person Saul was accountable to about the plans Jesus had spoken of: *"You will be a witness to all people of what you have seen and heard."*

Ananias baptized Saul, who then returned to Jerusalem. While Saul was praying in the temple, the Lord called him to leave Jerusalem immediately for his own safety. *"Go; I will send you far away to the Gentiles!"*

Saul was a new man. Eventually he changed his name to Paul and began a new life and ministry, taking the Gospel to the Gentiles. He would go on to write much of the New Testament. But the conversation on that Damascus road continued to influence his understanding of Jesus and discipleship. When he wrote to the church in Corinth, he gave a picture to describe God's people, the church.

> Now you are the body of Christ, and each one of you
> is a part of it.
>
> —1 Corinthians 12:27

A CLEAR WAY FORWARD

When we are in the process of repentance, we look for a clear way forward. If we are going to make significant changes in our lives, we want to be sure of the choices and the steps we take. This next stage of the Learning Circle is where clarity on a situation takes shape and propels us to take steps of faith.

Throughout the Bible we see that people worked out what God was saying in the context of ordinary community life. In the Old Testament, elders sat at the city gates. Their role was to help people work through what God was saying and doing in the events of their lives.

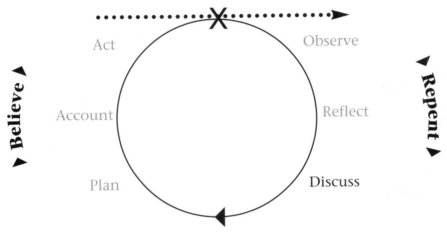

When we look at the Gospels we see that Jesus, like all rabbinical teachers of his day, used discussion as a way of training his disciples. On a trip from Galilee toward the villages of Caesarea Philippi, Jesus asked the disciples, "Who do people say I am?" (Mark 8:27).

The disciples shared the various answers they had heard from the crowds.

"Some say John the Baptist."

"Some say Elijah."

"One of the prophets."

> **IF WE ARE GOING TO MAKE SIGNIFICANT CHANGES IN OUR LIVES, WE WANT TO BE SURE OF THE CHOICES AND THE STEPS WE TAKE.**

"And what about you guys?" Jesus asked. "Who do you say that I am?"

Obviously Jesus wasn't suffering from an identity crisis. He knew exactly who he was! He was allowing the group discussion to bring his disciples to a clear understanding of who he was. This understanding would produce the confidence they needed for how they would live their lives in the years to come.

Peter, arguably the most outspoken of the disciples, responded, "You are the Messiah."

As the conversation continued, Jesus explained that Peter's response was not just about human words, but was revelation

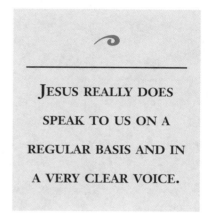

JESUS REALLY DOES SPEAK TO US ON A REGULAR BASIS AND IN A VERY CLEAR VOICE.

that God had given him. Notice that this revelation did not come out of a time of intense prayer and study. Peter's revelation and declaration of Jesus as Messiah came from a discussion as Jesus and his team were walking and talking together. Think about this for a second. Are your conversations with God a repetitive drone of requests for God to serve you and to help you and to bless you? Or do you spend time with God in the car or on a hiking trip or during your lunch break, talking to him, asking him questions, and listening for what he has to say? Jesus really does speak to us on a regular basis and in a very clear voice if we just take the time to be with him, to discuss life with him, and to listen to him.

When the New Testament church saw Gentiles become followers of Jesus, there was a lot of confusion. Some believed that the Gentiles needed to be circumcised in order to be saved. So believers from Judea traveled to Antioch and Syria to bring this new teaching.

Others, such as Paul and Barnabas, disagreed, surely believing that Jesus' message was far greater than circumcision. In the end, Paul and Barnabas traveled to Jerusalem to meet with the elders and apostles to get clarity on this issue. Different opinions were shared. Peter told of how God had called him to share the Gospel with Gentiles. It seemed strange to him to make the Gentiles carry the burdens of Jewish laws, when they had all—even the Jews—been saved by grace. Paul and Barnabas told the stories of what God had been doing amongst the Gentiles.

RECEIVING GOD'S GUIDANCE IN A COMMUNITY CONTEXT WAS A COMMON PRACTICE OF THE NEW TESTAMENT CHURCH.

A clearer understanding of God's perspective was emerging. As a result, James (the leader of the church in Jerusalem) concluded that circumcision of Gentiles was not necessary. He also gave guidelines about sexual immorality and cultural practices that would have made it hard for Jews and Gentiles to eat together. This decision shaped the church's attitude toward Gentiles and mission from that day onward. Again God's will was revealed through conversation.

Receiving God's guidance in a community context was a common practice of the New Testament church. When Paul wrote to the church in Corinth about how they would get an understanding of what God was saying, he said:

> Two or three prophets should speak, and the others should weigh carefully what is said.
>
> —1 Corinthians 14:29

Perhaps what Paul had in mind was the idea of elders at the gate. His culture had always developed and sharpened what God said in conversation with others. Believers in God sought the discernment of others in working out how God was leading.

It seems that in the Western world we are rediscovering the healing and empowering qualities of being part of a wider community. Our emerging culture expresses a desire to re-create community, with environments that provide space for discussion. People gather in coffeehouses and wine bars. They gather in chat rooms in cyberspace.

> COMMUNITY HELPS BRING CLARITY. AND WHEN WE HAVE A SENSE OF CLARITY ABOUT THE NEXT STEP, WE GROW IN CONFIDENCE.

Have you noticed how much time young people, in particular, spend in these places? Young adults are very often in the position of trying to work out what to do with their lives. These environments give people the opportunity to simply talk about where their lives are.

Learners like you and I need to get into the practice of discussion. As we bring our reflections to a community setting—a few trusted friends, a life group, our families, or our work teams—we can learn to discover how God is guiding us. Community helps bring clarity. And when we have a sense of clarity about the next step, we grow in confidence.

When I arrived in Phoenix, Arizona, I had no idea of how to get anywhere. Thankfully I'd worked out that I needed to drive on a different side of the road than what I was used to. But I had no idea where I was going. Obviously I didn't tell my wife, Sally, that, but you know how it is! I didn't have a clear sense of direction, so I wasn't confident. After I had lived in Phoenix for a few months, I had traveled to church so many times I could do it with my eyes closed. Now I know all the shortcuts and scenic routes. It's all clear to me, so I am confident behind the wheel.

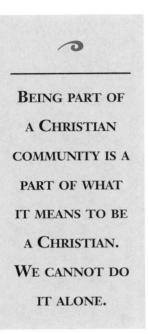

BEING PART OF A CHRISTIAN COMMUNITY IS A PART OF WHAT IT MEANS TO BE A CHRISTIAN. WE CANNOT DO IT ALONE.

Clarity takes us further than just confidence. Sometimes as we go through the Learning Circle, we realize that we need to take major steps that are daunting. We may need to change our jobs, move to a new place, or make a decision that will impact family life as we know it. As we face challenges like these, we need courage. It's hard to be courageous when we are unsure of what we are doing. Yet when we get a clear sense of how God is leading us, we have both confidence and courage. This is the biblical context for discussion.

Community leads to clarity.

Clarity gives us confidence.

When we are confident we can be courageous.

LEARNING IN COMMUNITY

As Christians we emphasize that our quiet time is one of the primary places where we receive guidance and direction from God. The other place where we expect to receive direction is from the preacher in the pulpit. Both these things are crucial parts of our walk with Jesus. If we are to grow in our relationship with Jesus, then like all other relationships we need to invest time. Likewise, we need to gather with other believers to worship God together and to listen to his Word. However, we cannot ignore the fact that when Jesus taught his disciples, discussion was a vital ingredient to learning how to apply kingdom principles to everyday life. If it's true for them, why wouldn't it be true for us too?

In the New Testament, people didn't just go to church; they were the church. They shared their possessions, resources, time, and decisions. They lived life together. This might seem a painful prospect. Many of us have become disillusioned by church splits or broken relationships and just don't want to go there again. Nonetheless, we are missing a vital part of our discipleship when we remain in isolation. Being part of a Christian community is a part of what it means to be a Christian. We cannot do it alone; we are the body of Christ and each one of us is a part of it.

GOD COULD BE TRYING TO COMMUNICATE SOMETHING WITH US AND WE'RE MISSING IT!

This stage of the Learning Circle can present many challenges.

It seems that we are living completely the opposite of how we were designed.

In today's culture we put a high value on privacy. Over the years we have learned to eat alone, work alone, be entertained alone, and live alone. And when we need to take a break, we can get drive-through coffee! We are in an environment where we can hear the Gospel of Christ, receive regular spiritual input, and even give to a church or ministry without moving from the couch. Perhaps we have become used to following Jesus alone.

Instead of living in a community that enables discussion with others, we have divided life into compartments. As if to confirm this, my house is surrounded by brick walls that are six feet high! I can't see my neighbors, let alone talk to them.

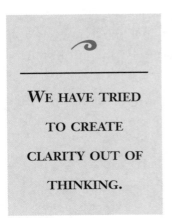

WE HAVE TRIED TO CREATE CLARITY OUT OF THINKING.

We have our family life in one box, our spiritual life in another. In yet another box is the time we spend at work. But life lived in compartments can get confusing.

It's easy to get used to thinking that it's us against the world. Think about your workplace. If there is no sense of community there (our friendships may exist in another box), then there's just a job to be done. It can feel like running around in the dark because no one communicates with anyone else. People are just getting on with their jobs. No one really knows anyone else or what they do well enough to appreciate what people bring to the team. As workers move around trying to be effective, they bump into each other. Misunderstandings happen, and people feel undermined. Someone is not consulted about a decision in which that person has years of experience and frustration flares. Another feels under constant pressure of unrealistic expectations. Constant complaining makes this person feel devalued. Everyone is disillusioned, and the confusion leads to conflict that divides. It's not long before the work group arrives at crisis point.

This could be true of our work, but also of our families and even of our churches.

Community + Clarity = Confidence and Courage.

Or

Compartments + Confusion = Conflict and Crisis.

Which would you prefer? We have tried to create clarity out of thinking. We think about our *kairos* and think and think and think. Finally, we think we have the answers and we think we've changed. But then what? We go through it all over again, only to tell ourselves we need to think about what we can do differently. Lean not on your own understanding ... it's really that simple. God created us to live and share life with each other.

Perhaps we have even reached the point where we accept compartments as the norm for family life. It's difficult to explain decisions about work to spouses or children, so we don't try anymore. It's awkward to ask children about events at school or their life with God. We hope that the youth pastor will do that. Or we somehow conclude that we shouldn't be talking about things, that family members need their space instead. As a result we are in danger of becoming strangers living under one roof. We need to be talking things through in families, with our colleagues, with friends, in our groups at church. God could be trying to communicate something with us and we're missing it!

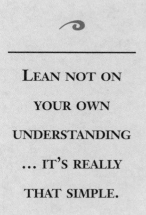

LEAN NOT ON YOUR OWN UNDERSTANDING ... IT'S REALLY THAT SIMPLE.

The film *Spanglish*[1] tells the story of Flor, a young Mexican woman who is a housekeeper to the Claskys, an affluent Los Angeles family. Flor is increasingly disturbed by the impact the family (especially the mother, Deborah Clasky) is having on her own bright twelve-year-old daughter, Cristina. Cristina's values and

---

1. James L. Brooks, *Spanglish*, DVD, directed by James L. Brooks (Culver City, Calif.: Columbia/TriStar Pictures, 2004).

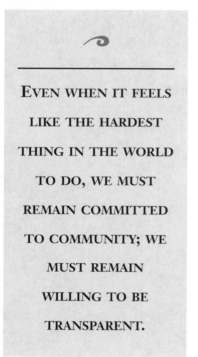

> **EVEN WHEN IT FEELS LIKE THE HARDEST THING IN THE WORLD TO DO, WE MUST REMAIN COMMITTED TO COMMUNITY; WE MUST REMAIN WILLING TO BE TRANSPARENT.**

outlook are changing, and Flor fears that her daughter is losing touch with her Mexican heritage.

Much to Cristina's horror, Flor quits her job (to avoid an affair with Deborah's husband) and tells Cristina that she will be leaving the private school that Deborah arranged for her to attend. Cristina is devastated. She screams at her mother, crying as she follows her down the street. As they arrive at the bus stop, Flor turns toward her daughter to try to console her. Cristina turns away and says, "I need my space," a comment Flor often heard around her former employer's home. Flor moves to within millimeters of Cristina's face and responds, "No space between us!"

Flor recognizes the need for community within her own family. It's hard, especially with teenagers like Cristina, to maintain open and honest dialogue about the significant experiences and questions of life. But sometimes, even when it feels like the hardest thing in the world to do, we must remain committed to community; we must remain willing to be transparent to those we spend our lives with.

MAL'S STORIES

One of our family disciplines is to eat together around the table when we are all in! The evening meal has become our touchstone point and a great time to catch up. Applying the Circle to our mealtimes has taught our children to identify *kairos* moments for themselves. Therefore over supper we normally do "best bit, worst bit" around the table. Each person shares the best and worst bits of the day. We find out much more about school, teachers, love interests, and what's really going on than we would if weren't intentional about it.

Sometimes we need to take the identified *kairos* for that person around the Circle as a family right then and there. A hot or emotive issue needs an accountability plan pretty quick! Since we're a competitive family, each person chooses who will share next. The last person gets a resounding cheer and has to go first the next time. When we've had visitors who have stayed for a while, we normally do "best bit, worst bit" of their stay, which helps us all to identify and process the *kairos* of that season together.

We also wanted to apply the principles of the Circle to how we discipline our children and resolve conflict as a family. We didn't want to send children to their rooms—that seemed like a reward, not a punishment. It also sends a message of isolation rather than acceptance. It is important for us to process the issue within the family as a family. Therefore we decided that we would specifically apply the Circle with our children by using the concept of

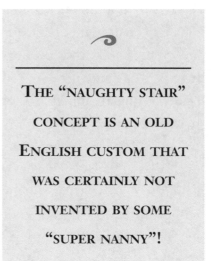

THE "NAUGHTY STAIR" CONCEPT IS AN OLD ENGLISH CUSTOM THAT WAS CERTAINLY NOT INVENTED BY SOME "SUPER NANNY"!

the "naughty stair." (On a side note, the "naughty stair" concept is an old English custom that was certainly not invented by some "super nanny"!)

The naughty stair is a spot in a neutral area of the house (not one person's favorite space). Right now it's a stair nearest to our kitchen. In another (very old) house, it was the top stair down to the cellar. If one of our kids does something that is a defining negative event—disobedience, evasiveness, etc.—we send the child to the naughty stair. We give him or her time there specifically to look (Observe) and think about (Reflect) what has happened. Then we'll go join the child on the stair to talk about it (Discuss). The child only leaves the stair when dealing with the consequences (Acting on a plan). It could be that he or she simply needs to say "sorry" to another member of the family.

After a while we found that if two children were squabbling we could send them to the naughty stair as a neutral space to sort out the issue (using their understanding of the Circle as the process). We call this application of Discuss getting "step time." Those two (or more!) involved can't leave the stair until they have a plan to, at the very least, forgive one another. Normally, they don't want to rake over the ashes of the *kairos;* they just get to the hugging and forgiving bit pretty quickly! If two of our children have had an argument, we often find them choosing to give themselves step time!

One thing we weren't expecting was the implications of step time for us as parents! One day when my wife and I got a little dramatic about a particular issue, our then five-year-old came in and sent us both to do some step time. After the initial shock we realized that if we were going to be true to applying this, we needed to comply. Being adults who don't forgive so quickly, we continued discussing our observations and reflections, with the door being opened on us every few minutes and our kids asking, "Have you forgiven each other yet?"

MIKE'S STORIES

As a family we have made a habit of talking through the big and small details of life, and we have learned to take note of the Lord leading us through our discussions. Meals have always been a time when we talk together, but there have been occasions when we needed to work through a big issue. This took more than a mealtime.

When it came to big decisions, such as moving to a new home, job, or country, we would have a family conference. Sally and I have always wanted the children to learn how to hear God for themselves. So even when our children were small, we encouraged them to talk with God about our life decisions so that we could discuss them properly as a family.

> **AS A RESULT OF THE DISCUSSION PROCESS, OUR CHILDREN HAD THE CONFIDENCE AND THE COURAGE TO TAKE A BIG STEP, CERTAIN THAT GOD WAS LEADING THEM.**

We had been living in Arkansas for about two and a half years. We were happy and settled as a family. One day I received a letter asking whether I would like to apply for the role of senior pastor at St. Thomas' Church in Sheffield, England. It was completely unexpected but we felt it was right to explore it as a possibility.

We traveled to England for an interview, and I was offered the job. But as far as the family was concerned, we needed to talk things through with the children, to check if this really was the direction God was leading us. We had a family conference and led the children through the process of looking at our lives to see what God was saying. Talking it through together, we told our children that there was a possibility we could move back to England and asked them how they felt about it.

Beccy, who was nine at the time, said, "I was always going to move back to England anyway." Clearly she was way ahead of us!

Libby, age seven, had practical questions. "What kind of house will we live in?"

Sam was only about four years old, but he was part of the discussion process. "Will I be nearer to my grandparents?"

It was time to pray, and we encouraged the children to listen to God. We also encouraged them to think through the things they would want God to provide if it was right to move.

After a while we got back to talking. One of the girls wanted God to provide friends; the other wanted to continue with horse riding. Sam wanted to spend time with his grandparents.

The family conference took about two hours. We talked and prayed, listened and talked. At the end of the conference, Sally and I were confident that a move to Sheffield was right for us as a family, but more importantly for us, the children were confident, too. As a result of the discussion process, our children had the confidence and the courage to take a big step, certain that God was leading them.

Ten years later, we found ourselves in a similar position. It appeared to us that God was calling us back to the States, this time to Arizona. It was time for another family conference, but this time it took place at Burger King! By this time Beccy was nineteen, Libby was seventeen, and Sam was thirteen.

We were used to hanging out together as a family and listening for God's direction as we talked. We explained the thoughts we'd had so far. Beccy, who had recently returned to Sheffield to start college after serving at a church in another part of England, shared, "When I was praying about moving back to Sheffield, God told me that it wasn't about you guys being here, but that he had called me back. I think God may have been preparing me for this."

Libby was at a crucial stage of her education, studying for exams that would help her progress to college. "I think it's right for you to go," she said. "And if you need to go now, you are free to go."

Sam was excited about the opportunity to go to a new place. But he also felt that if it was right, we wouldn't just go as a family—we would go with a wider team.

DISCUSSION CREATES THE CLARITY WE NEED AND GIVES US CONFIDENCE.

We had lots to work through. It was becoming clear that Arizona was right, but we needed more clarity. We continued to talk about the implications of such a move. Perhaps in our discussion God would help us understand what would help each of our children through this process.

Beccy knew it was right for her to stay in Sheffield, but she needed somewhere to live. Knowing that I would be back in Sheffield on a regular basis, we concluded it was important to have a base, so we would buy a house. Libby was given different options. We could help her go to college in the United States or in the United Kingdom. It was her choice. As we talked it through, Libby felt it was right to study in the United Kingdom. Sam was already keen on the idea of moving, so we talked through things like school and sports he loved, but we also took on board the word God gave us through Sam about moving to America with a team. It turned out that the team that joined us from Sheffield included all of Sam's godparents! In fact, all of the children have at least one godparent based in Phoenix.

Moving to Phoenix has been an exciting adventure for us as a family. Inevitably, change can be difficult, even for the most adventurous! But even when it's hard, each member of our family has something to hold on to: a clear indication of God directing our lives.

Whether it's as part of the family, at work, or in fellowship with other believers, discussion is the place where our process of repentance really takes shape. By the end of that journey we discover that we have that faith that comes from hearing the Word of God.

Discussion creates the clarity we need and gives us confidence. When we face challenges, we have the faith to act courageously. This leads us naturally to the next part of the Learning Circle. We have received direction. Now it's time for the changes on the inside to affect our daily lives. And it starts with a plan.

CHAPTER 9

Sounds Like a Plan

◠

*G*od warned the people of Israel. Again and again he spelled out for them the consequences of walking out of relationship with him. It was not going to be pretty. He sent prophets to make sure the people got the message loud and clear and to encourage them back to a faithful love for him. But the leaders, the priests, and the people had made up their own minds. So God did what he said he would do. God lifted his hand of protection from his people and they were caught up in the strivings for world dominance.

Assyrians invaded the northern part of the Jewish kingdom— Israel—and carried its people into exile. Judah—the southern kingdom—survived intact for more than a century until the Babylonians arrived. At that time, Jerusalem was destroyed and the temple of God was burned to the ground. Many people were killed; others were captured and taken to Babylon as slaves.

Many years later, Cyrus of Persia swept in and defeated the Babylonians. The Jewish people were released from slavery and given permission to return to Jerusalem. Under the leadership of

Zerubbabel the priest, those who chose to return to Jerusalem would rebuild the temple of God.

Eighty-one years passed.

Ezra and Zerubbabel led a group of two thousand people from Persia to Jerusalem to restore the temple. When they arrived, Ezra found that the people had lost sight of their relationship with God again, so he led them in a spiritual restoration.

Thirteen years passed.

Nehemiah was the cupbearer to King Artaxerxes I. He had the unenviable task of tasting the king's wine to make sure it wasn't poisoned! But his position also meant that he was one of the king's most trusted advisers.

Hanani, a fellow Jew, visited Nehemiah in Susa and told him about the state of Jerusalem. The city was in ruins socially, physically, and spiritually. The wall of Jerusalem that was meant to provide security from her enemies had been torn down and the gates burned to the ground.

Nehemiah was devastated by the news. He couldn't reply to what Hanani had to say. All he could do was sit down and cry.

Nehemiah didn't have to do anything about the news he heard. Wine tasting aside, he lived a comfortable life in the palace. Even though he had grown up as an exile in a foreign land, he was now in a place of honor and respect. Jerusalem was a ruined city that lay some nine hundred miles away, and Nehemiah had never even been there. He would have to start all over again. And even if Nehemiah did want to go, would the king let him?

The news about Jerusalem broke Nehemiah's heart. Even though he had never been there, this was still his homeland, the land of his heritage. Nehemiah wept, fasted, and prayed for days, asking God to do something.

The king knew his cupbearer well. Nehemiah was in such distress that he couldn't hide it. When the king noticed a troubled expression on Nehemiah's face and asked what was wrong, Nehemiah took a chance and told the king about Jerusalem.

God's hand was at work. Not only did the king give Nehemiah permission to go to Jerusalem, but he also gave him the resources to rebuild the city walls, the temple gate, and a house for himself! Nehemiah was on his way.

Nehemiah arrived in Jerusalem and stayed for three days, watching and waiting. Under the anonymity of darkness he went out at night to look at the city more closely. He inspected the walls and the gates. Nehemiah didn't tell anyone of his plans for Jerusalem, even those who traveled with him. Instead, he spent time observing and reflecting upon the needs of the city.

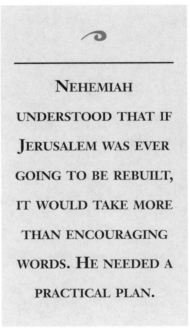

NEHEMIAH UNDERSTOOD THAT IF JERUSALEM WAS EVER GOING TO BE REBUILT, IT WOULD TAKE MORE THAN ENCOURAGING WORDS. HE NEEDED A PRACTICAL PLAN.

Soon it was time to share his reflections with the city officials.

"We all know the trouble we are in. Jerusalem is in a mess. The gates and the walls that are supposed to protect her have been burned down. But we can do something about this! Let's rebuild Jerusalem's walls and restore our city's pride!"

Nehemiah continued by telling them his experience of God's favor and his conversation with King Artaxerxes. The officials were inspired. "That sounds good. Let's start rebuilding." And they got right to work.

Enter Sanballat, Tobiah, and Geshem. These three were officials who did not like the Israelite people or anyone who tried to help them. They publicly ridiculed the people who were engaged in building the walls. When they saw that strategy was not working, they threatened to attack the workers.

The workers were tired. Standing in rubble up to their necks made it seem like rebuilding a wall was impossible. And they were intimidated by the threats of the opposition. They wanted to rebuild the wall, but they knew they couldn't defend themselves against so many enemies.

Nehemiah understood that if Jerusalem was ever going to be rebuilt, it would take more than encouraging words and the permission of the city officials. He needed a practical plan. This plan would have to empower the Israelite people and deal with their enemies. It had to enable them to carry on with the practicalities of building the wall, as well as strengthen their identity as God's people. So Nehemiah started putting his ideas to work.

> **INSTEAD OF FOCUSING ON DISCOURAGEMENT AND DESPAIR, THE PEOPLE FOCUSED ON THE PLAN.**

Nehemiah placed armed guards at the weakest points of the wall. He stationed others to stand and protect families that were working. After doing an inspection, he called the people together and explained the plan.

"Don't be afraid of your enemies. Remember God, your God, is bigger than they are and on your side. This is the time we fight. We fight for our families, for our friends, for our homes!"

Half of the people got back to work on the wall. The other half wore armor and stood guard with spears, shields, bows, and spears.

Every worker received a weapon. Even those who were working carried building materials in one hand and a weapon in the other. A trumpeter stayed with Nehemiah at all times, ready to sound the alarm if needed.

Nehemiah spoke to all the people again, explaining the next stage of the plan.

"Our work is so spread out that we are separated from each other along the wall. So we need to be alert. If you hear the sound of the trumpet, stop what you are doing and run to wherever the sound is coming from. It will be the sound of war, and our God will fight on our side!"

The people worked as a team from sunrise to sunset. Whenever people worked on the walls, others stood guard. Nehemiah told all the people living outside the city wall to move into Jerusalem so that more people were available to work and stand guard. Instead of focusing on discouragement and despair, the people focused on the plan. They carried their weapons everywhere, even if they were fetching water. They were ready.

After dealing with the threats to the people of Jerusalem that came from outsiders, Nehemiah had to address the conflicts that existed within the Israelite community itself. The physical walls may have been rebuilt, but the social and spiritual walls of the Israelite community were still in desperate need of restoration.

The poor in the community were being oppressed by the rich. The interest rates they were charged on loans was so high that they had to mortgage their homes and fields and even sell their children into slavery just to survive. Nehemiah was angry and called a public meeting to call the rich and the officials in the community to account.

Nehemiah reminded them that as God's people they had responsibilities to look out for one another, not to oppress their most vulnerable citizens. He gave an account of how up until this point he had loaned resources to those in need, but it was time to move forward as a community. The loans would stop, and so would the extortion.

Nehemiah and the Israelites doggedly pursued the vision to rebuild the city and the temple at Jerusalem. Opposition was never far away, but the Israelites would not be moved. As the governor of the region, Nehemiah continued to act upon the vision to restore Jerusalem on every level. Rebuilding the wall closed the door to Israel's enemies and opened up opportunities for the restoration of the people. He appointed leaders who would govern and protect Jerusalem with integrity. He organized the community in their families to restore a sense of identity. He worked alongside Ezra to restore the worship life of the Israelites and to reestablish their relationship with God.

When the wall of Jerusalem was dedicated to God, the people held a huge celebration. In fact, it was such a big party that the joy of the people could be heard for miles. A new day dawned.

WHAT'S YOUR HURRY?

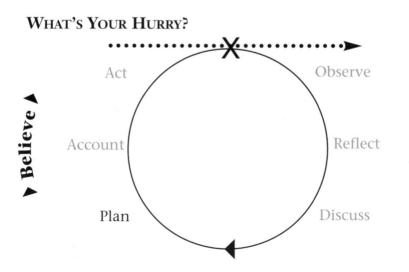

Discussion—the final stage of repentance—presents us with the chance to bring clarity and focus to the changes God wants to bring to our lives.

But what happens next? Remember, faith is not a private thing—it's public. It is where our certainty or confidence begins to shape how we live our lives.

You might be tempted after observation, reflection, and discussion to jump right into action. Repentance has shown us how we need to change. God has challenged us, and we can see the kingdom opportunities in every part of our lives. We are ready to see the kingdom come, so let's do it!

You want to be a better spouse, so you book a meal for two at an exclusive restaurant. You know you need to spend more time with the children, so let's do that right now. You have become aware of the need to be a Christian example at work, so let's get right to it.

So you tell your wife about dinner, but she reminds you that you have an important parent-teacher conference the same night—and she has reminded you about that conference every day for the past week. You tell your children that you want to hang out with them all weekend, but they are all at sleepovers at their friends' houses. They asked your permission, you said yes, and now it looks like you have changed your mind. Your enthusiasm just comes across as pressure to do something they don't want to do. And your work colleagues? You invite someone to church and the person expresses a hatred of organized religion, and you have no idea what to say next! Well, that went well, didn't it?

You were trying to live a passionate life and all you managed to do was confuse your wife, annoy your children, and alienate your work colleagues! Great!

The first stage of faith is not "Just do it!" The first step is to make a plan.

GOD, THE MASTER PLANNER

For some of us, planning doesn't seem like a faith-filled activity. We equate faith with bungee-jumping or skydiving—a risk factor is essential. However, faith isn't spelled r-i-s-k; it's spelled s-u-r-e. Many great projects of the Bible could not have been accomplished without a plan:

• The exodus under Moses.
• The conquest of the land under Joshua.
• Building the temple under Solomon.
• Rebuilding the walls of Jerusalem led by Nehemiah.
• Paul's mission to the Gentiles.

These projects were huge activities where God's kingdom came in power and all these projects needed a plan. Planning is part of God's character—he is a God of order, not chaos. Jeremiah 29:11 tells us that God has plans for each of us—plans with a very specific purpose and intent.

The Gospels give us glimpses into Jesus' practice of planning. Observing the reactions of the crowds and the religious leaders in relation to what his Father was doing, he directed and redirected his plans. According to plan Jesus kicked off his earthly ministry with forty days in the wilderness, he arrived at Lazarus's grave days after Lazarus died, and he made his final journey to Jerusalem. Jesus constantly guided his disciples through plans. Some were short and simple:

> But seek first his kingdom and his righteousness, and all these things will be given to you as well.
> Therefore do not worry about tomorrow, for tomorrow will worry about itself. Each day has enough trouble of its own.
>
> —Matthew 6:33–34

Other plans were more detailed. Jesus sent seventy-two disciples out into the local towns and cities as preparation for his visit, giving them specific instructions:

> After this the Lord appointed seventy-two others and sent them two by two ahead of him to every town and place where he was about to go. He told them, "The harvest is plentiful, but the workers are few. Ask the Lord of the harvest, therefore, to send out workers into his harvest field. Go! I am sending you out like lambs among wolves. Do not take a purse or bag or sandals; and do not greet anyone on the road. "When you enter a house, first say, 'Peace to this house.'"
>
> —Luke 10:1–5

When it comes to planning, many of us think that we are no good at it. We read the books and attend the seminars and get disillusioned with how bad we are at planning. It's no wonder we never seem to achieve our goals! But the reality is that we make lots of plans every day. How do we get the kids ready for school? How do we manage the commute to work? If we didn't make plans we wouldn't make it out of bed in the morning. From the moment we awake until the moment we crash into our beds and fall asleep, we make plans.

We make plans all the time!

Nehemiah was confident that God wanted the walls of Jerusalem rebuilt. He had faith that God wanted to do something new for the people of Jerusalem. His faith produced specific plans that would lead toward fulfilling his vision.

As we enter the process of faith, specific plans take us closer to seeing the kingdom of God at work in our lives.

PROCESSED *P*s

Many consultants and practitioners in various professions are really good at developing plans for every occasion and circumstance. Such "prepackaged" plans can be helpful, if only to serve as models of what a plan looks like. However, there's nothing more effective than a plan you've developed yourself. No one knows better than you what God is saying to you through the parts of the Learning Circle. So learning to develop your own plan is important. Here's a useful tool to help you get started: Processed *P*s. Each stage of the process begins with the letter *P*. As you go through each *P* your decisions begin to take shape and build toward the plan you want to make.

When most people think about putting a plan together, it often becomes very overwhelming because we tend to see the overall "big picture" of the plan—carrying out the plan starts to look very complicated and it's simply to hard to formulate. However, if we can learn to break down our plan into its individual parts it becomes quite simple. That is the idea behind Processed *P*s. Each *P* is simply a result of the previous *P*. They flow together, one to the other, and are connected to each other. As we look at each *P*, you will begin to see how you can form a detailed and dynamic plan by simply beginning with your own personal thoughts and beliefs and carrying those through to the next logical step.

PRINCIPLES

Your firmly held personal values—your principles—are sometimes hard to put into words. Perhaps your *kairos* event has highlighted that you are too busy for your family. You spend a lot of time in the office, and you are tired when you get home. You try to grab time with your spouse, and it feels like the only time you talk to your kids is in the car, driving them to their various activities.

When you look back on your own childhood, you were frustrated that you never got any time with your own parents. You'd like to do things differently.

Your plan should take into consideration and reflect what you value most. Is family more important to you than advancing your career? Are there personal activities you are willing to sacrifice for that extra time with your spouse or child? What do your finances show about what you value most? We use our principles—what we believe in and value—to guide us as we explore the specific purposes we have for implementing a particular plan.

PURPOSE

If you want to make a plan, you need to define its purpose. You may have intentions about a general issue or about a specific project in your life. Purpose is the reason behind your actions, your ambitions, your aspirations. It's what you want to see when the dust clears, when the sun sets, when the hay and stubble are burned away. Purpose can motivate us, but God's plan for us is that we have a hope and a future.

Maybe your hope is that when your children are adults they will look back and have lots of good memories of the times you spent together as a family. Some things could be big events, others could be small, but they would be heartwarming memories. Perhaps your purpose is to give your children a sense of family that you lacked growing up. Your purpose might also include your desire to be a witness to others about what God's Word instructs on family

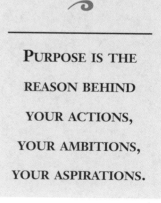

PURPOSE IS THE REASON BEHIND YOUR ACTIONS, YOUR AMBITIONS, YOUR ASPIRATIONS.

relationships. Upon the discovery and evaluation of your plan's purpose, you will naturally start to define and order the list of priorities that come up in the development of your plan. With your principles and your purpose firmly in place, your priorities will clearly reveal themselves.

PRIORITIES

We all have priorities—spoken or unspoken, recognized or hidden—that shape our lives. When you look at a project you want to launch or a dream you hope to accomplish, your priorities are the things you want to examine first. These can be emotional or rational. Simply put, your priorities are the things your principles and purpose deem important or not important in the process of carrying out your plan! You may find in the process of repentance that God shows you what you need to prioritize. Over the years I have learned some basic priorities that have become the foundations of my life. God comes first, then Sally, then the children. My wife and family are my primary calling. After that comes my calling as a church leader, then my career.

As you look at your priorities, you may realize that you have been expressing your family as a priority through your job. You work hard to provide for all their needs. Then through your *kairos* God reveals to you that the family needs your presence more than your paycheck. The first thing you want to do is to look at how you can begin to make more time, how can you be more present in their daily lives.

Single or married, minister or business professional, the three dimensions of the *LifeShapes* Triangle can help you maintain a healthy balance in your priorities. Along with your principles and purpose, the three dimensions of Up, In, and Out can be foundational to your plan: God, Your Family and Church, Others. As your priorities begin to manifest themselves, you will begin to understand what you need to do—to practice—in order to make those priorities a reality. In other words: If (blank) is my priority, what do I need to do to make sure that is always at the top of my list?

Practices

Your practices are defined by your principles, your purpose, and your priorities. You never just start doing something without first examining all the reasons you have for doing it. For example, when you go on vacation with family, do you believe in time together or the opportunity to do things separately? Do you prefer an active holiday where you take your backpack and minimal supplies and go out into the great unknown? Or would you prefer to stay in a nice hotel by the beach where you can sunbathe and read a book? For family sanity, it's important to establish your preferred practices before the vacation!

Our churches have practices that reflect what they believe in. For example, at St. Thomas' Church, we established practices for praying for people. We trained members of the congregation to pray with people in a nonintrusive manner and with people of the same sex whenever possible. There is an element of practicality to practices—a melding

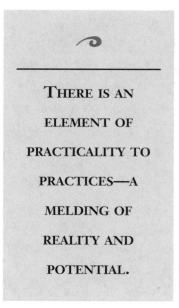

THERE IS AN ELEMENT OF PRACTICALITY TO PRACTICES—A MELDING OF REALITY AND POTENTIAL.

of reality and potential. It's one of the *P*s that makes the success of the plan possible. Finally, now that you have looked at all the individual pieces, you see how easy it is to form a complete plan.

PLAN

We've got our principles and our purpose in place. As a result, we know what our priorities are. Our priorities then shape what we need to do, what practices will work for our situation. The next *P* is the plan. To plan is simply to put these things on a timeline, to establish when the details of our plan (priorities, practices, etc.) will take place. Sometimes we hope things will fall into place, but without the timeline of when we intend to do something about all our *P*s, they are just ideas floating in the air.

The plan looks at when you intend to do something about your new God-given priorities, when you will begin to take up new practices of spending time with the family. It begins to bring your ideas into reality.

PRAY

Though I have put "pray" as the last *P*, we are actually praying all the way through this process. Your principles and purpose can be the result of your ongoing dialogue with your Father. He has reminded you of what you should be living for. Your priorities were shaped in those times of drawing near to God. Your practices and your plan reflect the changes God has worked in your heart. The *P*s show the crossover from repentance to faith. However, when we look at all we have put together in our overall plan, we return to prayer.

As you look at your plan, where are the gaps that you can't fill and that need to be covered by God's grace? Where do you need God to move in power? It may be a financial issue as you launch a new business. Or perhaps you are trying to organize your hectic schedule so that you can take a family vacation, but you need someone to take care of your workload in the office. Prayer opens up the conduit of God's power to fill in the gaps and enable the success of your plan.

You can apply the Processed *P*s to all areas of life, from moving to a new house to planning a wedding to starting up a new ministry. Don't be surprised or disappointed if you need to go through the Processed *P*s several times to work out what you are going to do. The results are worth it!

So you have a practical plan for the way forward. For some of us it is hard to get beyond our plans and our strategies for the future. You planned that vacation, but you never got around to taking it. You thought about moving to a new house, but then you got distracted by another event in the family. You looked into starting a new business, you even went to the bank, but all the papers are still on the desk. You've made plans before, but they did not seem to get anywhere. Why?

The problem is turning the plan into an action! That is where accountability comes in.

CHAPTER 10

Your Dad Is Trying to Kill Me!

*H*ow could something that started out so right go so wrong?

When he killed Goliath, David became a national hero overnight. King Saul exempted his family from taxes and promised his daughter's hand in marriage. David was going to be rich, very rich.

Saul sent David out to fight, and David always came home a champion. He was popular with the army and with the people. Everybody loved David. Jonathan, Saul's son, became his closest friend. Everything was falling into place.

One day King Saul and the army returned from battle. The women of the city came out to welcome their war heroes with singing and dancing. They sang: "Saul has slain his thousands and David his ten thousands."

Not good. Hero or not, no way was David going to get more credit than the king. Saul was livid.

Years before, Saul had gotten impatient for Samuel to arrive and had done the job of a priest himself. God rejected Saul for his disobedience, and the Spirit of God left the king. Saul was tormented by an evil spirit. The royal court watched helplessly as Saul moaned and howled in desperation. Horror would strike without warning, reducing the king to something far less dignified than his royal office. Nothing seemed to help. The royal court persuaded the king to listen to the soothing tones of a musician during these episodes. David had been selected to play his harp for the king. When David played, the evil spirit left Saul, and the king had some respite from the torment.

So Saul liked David. But this business of the people congratulating David more than the king himself was crossing the line.

Saul was in a particularly foul mood the day he returned from battle. A dark cloud hung over his head. David played his harp, and a calm gentle melody filled the room. Saul sighed deeply, and for a moment it appeared that the cloud over Saul might disperse. But not this time. He began to murmur under his breath. "I hate you. I hate you."

David, not quite sure of what Saul was saying, continued to play.

"I hate you!" Saul screamed, his eyes bulging with anger. He picked up his spear and hurled it at David. David jumped out of the way just in time and then ran for his life. He was reluctant to return to the palace and rightly so! This job was becoming uncomfortable. The next time David played, the same thing happened.

Saul continued to treat David badly. He sent David away from the palace and made him a captain over a smaller unit of Saul's army. It was an unexplained demotion. Then Saul offered his eldest daughter, Merab, in marriage—but changed his mind at the last minute. Saul eventually gave his daughter Michal to David but then ordered his servants and his son Jonathan to assassinate David. Jonathan managed to bring Saul to his senses, but only temporarily. As David played music for Saul, the king hurled his spear at him again. David ducked out of the way, and the spear stuck in the wall.

David escaped into the night. Nothing had changed!

David was on the run from Saul. Desperate, he sought out his friend Jonathan. All he has ever done was serve the king in the best way he knew how. So he asked Jonathan, "What have I done? Tell me what crime I committed! What did I do to your father that was so wrong that I deserve this? I don't want to sound disrespectful, but your dad is trying to kill me!"

The two men had an intense discussion. As far as David was concerned it was obvious: Saul had it in for him. Jonathan was sure that if that were true Saul would have told him about it. He had seen reconciliation between Saul and David before.

"Why would he tell you?" cried David, exasperated "He knows that we are friends! I swear to you, my life is on the line here. Your father wants me dead!"

Jonathan sat down and put his face in his hands. He couldn't ignore what David was saying. He had seen the way his father had changed. He had hoped it wouldn't come to this.

"Let's just make sure we've got our facts right," Jonathan said. "Tell me what you want me to do."

The friends devised a plan. It was the time of the new moon festival, and David would be expected at the palace. This time David would stay away. When the king asked for him, Jonathan would say that David was with his family. If Saul took it well, it would be a sign that all was well. If not, then David was right. Jonathan would let him know the next day.

As David began to walk into the fields, Jonathan stopped him.

"One more thing. I hope the Lord is with you like he once was with my father." Jonathan somehow knew that David was called to be king, even though as Saul's son, he himself was the heir to the throne. "But keep me as your covenant friend. And if for some reason, I die, then keep this covenant friendship with my family. When the Lord deals with all your enemies, remember this agreement!"

Jonathan returned to the palace.

Sadly for Jonathan, David was right. When Saul realized that David was away, he exploded. He cursed Jonathan.

"Don't you realize that as long as that boy lives, you will never be king? Now bring him to me, and I'll kill him!"

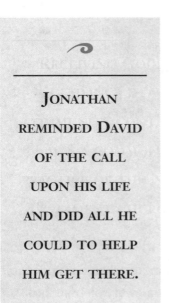

JONATHAN REMINDED DAVID OF THE CALL UPON HIS LIFE AND DID ALL HE COULD TO HELP HIM GET THERE.

When Jonathan tried to plead David's case, Saul threw his spear at him. Jonathan had seen and heard all he needed to. He stormed out of the room.

The next day Jonathan went out to the fields to meet David with the bad news. David was about to lose everything—his family, his wife, his livelihood, his home. He was about to lose his friend. David was absolutely crushed. Both men cried, but David cried the most.

Jonathan and David reaffirmed their commitment to one another as friends and then went their separate ways.

David spent years on the run from Saul. At one point Jonathan went to Horesh to meet him. Jonathan encouraged David to hold on tightly to his relationship with God.

"Don't be afraid; my father won't ever find you! You will be the king of Israel, David. That's God's plan for your life. You can trust what God has promised you. You can trust what God said to you through Samuel. He has confirmed it to you again and again. And

I shall be right there next to you! My father knows it." They renewed their covenant friendship before God.

It was the last time David and Jonathan ever saw each other. Both Saul and Jonathan fell in battle against the Philistines.

Many years later David was able to fulfill his part of his pact with Jonathan. David was now king over all Israel. Maybe David remembered old times, and he remembered an old friend. Maybe he reached for something on his table and he noticed the scar on the heel of his hand (the symbol of a covenant agreement) and he remembered Jonathan. Jonathan, the friend who encouraged and supported David through some of his darkest years, at great personal cost. Jonathan, who reminded David of the call upon his life and did all he could to help him get there.

"Is there anyone left of Jonathan's family that I can show kindness to, that I can fulfill my commitment to?"

David discovered that Jonathan had a son called Mephibosheth, who was five years old when his father died. When the news of Jonathan's death reached Jerusalem, Mephibosheth's nurse took the young boy and tried to take him to a place of safety. Tragically, as she was running with him, she dropped him and he became crippled as a result.

David had Mephibosheth brought to the palace. Mephibosheth, now a young man, was terrified. He would have learned from the cradle that David, this great and powerful king, was his enemy. David must want to eliminate all potential threats to the throne. He would surely get rid of Saul's grandson. Mephibosheth bowed before David to hear the king's verdict.

"Don't be afraid," said David. "I've not brought you here to hurt you. I've brought you here because your father was a friend to me. He shared his life with me and stood beside me. I want to remember the covenant agreement that he and I made."

David gave Mephibosheth the land that belonged to Jonathan and Saul, with servants who would look after the land. This gift set him up for life. He also arranged for Mephibosheth to eat at the palace with David's family. It was as though he were one of David's own sons.

It was clear from the early days that David was called to be king. There was something special about him, and God was with him in a powerful way. But there was no way he was going to get there on his own. It was Jonathan, who encouraged him, supported him, and even challenged him on occasions, who made all the difference. And David knew it. Jonathan held David accountable for the plans that David made and the overall plan both men knew God had in store for David.

OUR BEST INTENTIONS

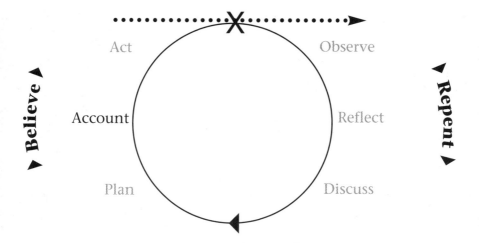

Our best plans often become little more than good intentions when we try to accomplish them on our own. How many of us have started a new year with intentions to spend more time with the children, lose weight, be nice to that difficult character at work, spend more time with God, stop speeding—only to have failed by the end of the first week?

If a plan is going to be effective, then we need at least one person who is going to hold us accountable for it. Faith is not a private thing and change does not take place in private. The changes that took place internally as we repented are revealed as we walk out a life of faith.

In a society where we value our independence and privacy so much, being accountable may seem like the last thing we want to do! Even in the church, we look up to "the rugged individual," the person who does things his or her way and manages to succeed. We may even aspire to become more self-sufficient. We would rather be independent than rely on anyone else for support or encouragement. Besides, aren't we supposed to depend on God? We don't want others to think badly of us, and we don't want to bother anyone else. Why should we burden someone else with our problems?

It may be that it's just hard to be open with other people about your life, your plans, your hopes, and your aspirations. You've always been a private person. It's just embarrassing to talk that way with other people.

Perhaps for some of us the idea of accountability is a complete turnoff. It sounds like giving up your freedom and giving someone else the opportunity to rule your life. Why would anyone in their right mind do that? Who wants to be controlled by someone who knows only as much as you anyway?

Before we just ignore this part of the Learning Circle, we need to clearly define what it is!

ACCOUNTABILITY IS ...

Accountability is not someone else telling you what to do. Accountability is *asking* another person to help you do the things you already want to do.

You've made the plan; you've just asked someone you can trust to help you stick to it. Accountability is the place where you share with someone the aspirations of your heart, plans, and goals. You invite that person to remind you of the plans you have made, the steps you want to take, and the things God has spoken to you.

Your relationship with this person is a cross between a cheer-leader and a coach. He or she will cheer you along your journey and like a coach will not be afraid to confront your weaknesses and challenge you.

For accountability to work, it must be based in a strong and trusting relationship. This is often a friendship with someone you have invested a great deal of your life and time in, but it also may be someone who serves as your mentor or spiritual guide, such as a pastor, church leader, or counselor. Our emphasis will be on accountability through friendship because that is the most common type of trust relationship. David and Jonathan could talk as honestly as they did because they were firm friends. David could trust and accept the challenges and guidance of Jonathan because he had no doubt that Jonathan wanted to see David receive all that God had for him. Why wouldn't he? He was his friend.

Jesus used the same pattern of accountability based on friendship with his disciples. After Peter denied even knowing Jesus, the first thing Jesus did when he reinstated him was to establish their friendship.

There can be no doubt that Peter felt like a failure. He had followed Jesus for three years and seen and experienced some amazing things. As one of the disciples in Jesus' intimate circle, he'd vowed that he would never deny Jesus. He was so wrong! What made it worse was that Peter knew he'd failed his friend. As they ate their last meal together, Jesus said to his disciples that the greatest kind of love was when someone laid down his life for his friends (John 15:13). He continued by saying that the disciples weren't his servants anymore. They were more than that; they were his friends.

After Jesus had been resurrected, he met some of the disciples who had decided to go out fishing by the Sea of Galilee. Peter was among them. After breakfast, Jesus took Peter aside and talked with him.

"Peter, do you love me?"

In English, we have only one common word for "love," while Greek has multiple words with multiple meanings. So we don't see in our translations that the first two times Jesus asked this question he is actually asking whether Peter loves him sacrificially, enough to lay down his life for him. Peter responds by saying he loves Jesus as a friend. Jesus then reminds Peter of his calling. Jesus asks Peter a third question—does Peter love him as a friend? Upset, Peter responds, "Lord, you know me and you know everything about me. You know I love you; you know I am your friend."

Now that the friendship has been reaffirmed, Jesus gives Peter a plan for the future for which Jesus will hold him accountable. "Feed my sheep."

WHO DO YOU TRUST?

So what about this friendship/mentorship thing? What if you're not really all that good at making friends? Maybe you have friends but none you're willing to open up to or trust with the details and longings of your life. Perhaps you feel uncomfortable even being that vulnerable with your spouse. For all our talk about relationships, friendships, and authenticity, there are many who still don't quite understand what it means to have a transparent relationship with someone.

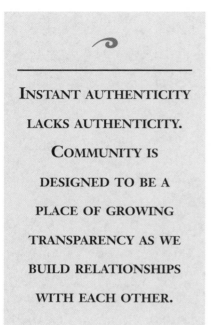

INSTANT AUTHENTICITY LACKS AUTHENTICITY. COMMUNITY IS DESIGNED TO BE A PLACE OF GROWING TRANSPARENCY AS WE BUILD RELATIONSHIPS WITH EACH OTHER.

In many ways, we have become so focused on authenticity that we begin to *expect* authenticity. As small groups form or as people meet in coffee shops for discussion, everyone comes in with the idea of instant authenticity, to be and share who they truly are, not just be fake like everyone else. While it's true that God created us to live in community and to share our lives with others, he did not create us to begin friendships by instantly dumping all our life onto someone else. Instant authenticity lacks authenticity. Community is designed to be a place of growing transparency as we build relationships with each other. As we invest in our community and relationships by spending time together in discussion, we widen the doors of transparency and authenticity through trust.

So, if transparency and accountability take place in a trust relationship such as a friendship or mentorship, how do we build and form and cultivate that relationship? How do we approach someone about starting a relationship with us that will lead to accountability? We begin by taking initiative. You will have to reach out in some way. Everybody is afraid of it—it doesn't matter who you are, whether you are outgoing or shy. Take a moment and think: Who can I reach out to and take initiative with? Next, you must be prepared to make the sacrifice of reaching out and identifying with another person. You find what you have in common with a potential friend and allow them to share something of your identity. Go beyond taking initiative and give the sacrifice that will begin to win a friend. In addition to sacrifice and initiative, friends show loyalty. That means you speak well of your friends when they're not around. You choose to defend them and speak the best about them. When people feel secure in a relationship, they become more open and are willing to give more of themselves.

As you continue to build your friendship/mentorship relationship, remember that true friends are not afraid to confront and challenge. Genuine friendships are not relationships where people simply agree not to say things that might upset each other. Authentic friendships are those where a friend can confront and challenge what has been said or done yet the friendship will not be risked. Another important factor to remember as you look for a friend is that friends give you the freedom to be yourself. It may not always be freedom without challenge and confrontation, but it is freedom to be who you are and what you are. The freedom to express yourself in whatever unique way comes to you! Friends give encouragement. A friend will speak God's word to you and that word will put courage in your heart. That word will never come as a put-down or criticism, but as a strengthening and healing message. Make sure that you are not only seeking that kind of friend, but also *being* that kind of friend. Finally, friends build memories. It is often the memories of friendships that carry people through hard times. Remembering a friendship as a place where you received God's blessing gives a strong assurance in times of need that you will receive that blessing again. Don't be afraid to build lasting memories that will carry you through difficult times. All of these qualities were lived out in the bond Jesus shared with his disciples, and you, too, can begin to live out friendship as God designed it.

GETTING INTO HUDDLES

Accountability was a way of life for the disciples. As disciples of Jesus, we need to learn how to develop the kind of friendships where we can invite our trusted friends to hold us accountable for the steps of faith we want to take. Like the first disciples, we need people who will help us live out the life of faith we want to live. We need those people in our lives who will cheer us on.

> Let us consider how we may spur one another on
> toward love and good deeds.
> —Hebrews 10:24

These people must also challenge us.

> Better is open rebuke than hidden love.
> Wounds from a friend can be trusted, but an enemy
> multiplies kisses.
> —Proverbs 27:5–6

When I was based at St. Thomas' Church in Sheffield, I was discipling a young team that would ultimately take over leadership of the church when I left. I wanted to find a way to mentor them effectively. We needed a regular venue for character, skill, and vision development. I looked at how other people were discipling young leaders in different parts of the world to see what we could apply to our situation. Unlike my generation, which viewed responsibility as a great honor, this emerging generation seemed to view it with some suspicion. They just didn't get excited about it in any way at all!

We met together as a team regularly, but we needed time where we would not just attend to business. So we met socially. Some of the team would play golf with me; others had meals with my family and me. At least once a month we would all go out together. Alongside this, we met weekly simply to be accountable for what God was doing in our lives. These became great times of fun and friendship, and as relationships deepened we worked through issues of taking responsibility.

We called these groups "huddles." We formed a list of questions we looked at every week to help us identify together what God was doing. Because we met so regularly, it meant that we were able to keep each other accountable about the progress we were (or weren't!) making.

The questions varied over the years. Eventually we came up with a list that looked at our relationship with God (Up), our relationship with other believers (In), and our relationship with the world around us (Out):

UP

- Do I make enough space for prayer?
- Do I pursue intimacy with Jesus?
- What is on my heart in intercession?
- Am I living in the power of the Spirit?
- Am I seeing personal revival?
- Do I still feel pleasure?
- Am I living in a state of peace?
- Am I afraid or nervous?
- Am I obedient to God's prompting?
- Do I keep my perspective?

IN

- Do I love the flock?
- Is time a blessing or a curse?
- Am I resting enough?
- How are my relationships with my friends?
- Am I experiencing intimacy in relationships?
- Do I keep my promises?
- How easy is it for me to trust people?
- Am I discipling others?
- Is my family happy?
- Am I sleeping and eating well?
- Am I making myself vulnerable to others?

OUT

- Do I have a heart for the lost?
- How often do I share my faith?
- Do I leave time for relationships with non-Christians?
- Am I running the race with perseverance?
- Do I have a vision?
- Am I dying to success?
- Am I proud or ashamed of the Gospel?
- Am I a servant?

Do I find it easy to recognize People of Peace?

Can I take risks?

We weren't out to embarrass each other or make someone feel bad. We were friends who wanted help in achieving our goals. We were prepared to be open, even vulnerable, to get there. We knew we had a safe arena to speak and to listen to what people had to say to us.

Huddles became part of the infrastructure of leadership training in our church. My team of leaders who were in my huddle had its own huddles of emerging leaders.

A WAY OF LIFE

In some situations a group of people is not the best place to go for the Account stage of the Learning Circle. In certain circumstances, accountability works best in same-sex groups of two or three people. This was the fabric of church life in St. Thomas' Church. People would gather with friends on a regular basis to talk and pray about the plans they had made to deal with certain issues. It could revolve around a particular temptation, a struggle they faced. And though it was a vulnerable and humbling experience, the group enabled people to walk through the journey of repentance and faith.

These accountability relationships are the kind of friendships we see in the example of David and Jonathan. They are relationships of encouragement and loyalty. They are relationships of freedom. We are not forced to be accountable, but we ask friends to help us by holding us accountable for our plans. These are relationships where challenge and confrontation happen, yet the future of the relationship is not at risk.

Disciples need accountability in their friendships. We need to get past our notions of privacy and begin to develop friendships where we can be open and honest and allow others to do the same. Openness is a key not only to effectiveness in ministry, but also to maintaining purity before God and those around us. It is a way to protect our marriages, our ethical behavior at work, and our family life.

If there is any area of your life you're not able to share with at least one other person, then you are more vulnerable in times of temptation. Sin tends to grow in darkness, and confession is the best way to bring light into our souls. Shame will keep us from sharing, but as disciples we need to get beyond this. We need to be free from any shadows of the past, free from any fears of exposure in the future. Even shame can find its roots in our pride. We don't want people (even our friends) to think less of us, for our image and reputation to be affected, so we keep things hidden. Accountable friendships are a place where you can

> ... confess your sins to each other and pray for each other so that you may be healed.
>
> —James 5:16

Sharing thoughts and even failures with another person is difficult for most of us, no matter how good a friend we are talking to. But it is a vital part of our growth.

If accountability is the weakest stage of the Learning Circle for you, then perhaps the best place to start is to look again at your friendships. Obviously not every person in our lives will be a close friend with whom we share our deepest secrets! But neither should every friend be little more than an acquaintance. Take the time to develop friendships and relationships that are open and honest. With lives as busy as most of ours are, this can be difficult to do, but it is always worthwhile.

The process of learning is almost complete. If we have learned how to observe, reflect, discuss, plan, and account, then the next stage is inevitable. It is time to act.

CHAPTER 11

And...Action!

*T*eacher, what do I need to do in order to get eternal life?"

Jesus looked at the man asking the question. He was well dressed, young, and passionate. This wasn't one of those trick questions the religious leaders used to try to trip up Jesus. This guy was really searching for answers.

"Well, you know how it works," Jesus began. "You live by the guidelines that God has already made clear to us. Don't murder, steal, and commit adultery. Don't tell lies. Honor your parents; love your neighbor as you love yourself."

But the young man was persistent. "I've done all of that. I've kept God's commandments. But there's something else—I just know there is. What am I missing?"

Jesus looked at the young man. He loved him! He loved the passion, the fire that burned in his heart and the enthusiasm to follow God. And Jesus knew exactly what he was missing.

"If you want to give your all ..."

"Yes!" The young man interrupted, nodding his head. "I do!"

"If you want to give your all," Jesus continued slowly, deliberately, "go and sell all that you have, give away all you've got to the poor. Your riches will be in heaven. And then come and follow me" (Matt. 19:16–22, author's paraphrase).

This wasn't what the young man was expecting to hear from Jesus. Sell everything? Give it all away? He wanted to follow Jesus—he really did. But not like this. He was a wealthy young man with a lot going for him; he didn't want to let that go. He wanted to have it all and he was devastated to discover that life didn't always work out like that. Slowly, sadly he nodded at Jesus. Looking at the ground, he walked away.

THEY HAD WATCHED HIS PASSION, AND THEY HAD SEEN THAT IT COULDN'T TAKE HIM ALL THE WAY.

Jesus let out a huge sigh. He was sad to see this young man go. The disciples with Jesus had been watching everything. Jesus turned to them and said: "It's so hard for rich guys like him to enter God's kingdom! It's easier for a camel to get through the eye of a needle than for the rich to enter the kingdom of God!"

The disciples were completely freaked out. They had seen this guy. He was one of the good ones! He was passionate, he wasn't cynical, and he wanted to know God better. In their eyes, he was already doing so many things right. He wasn't like Matthew, a corrupt tax collector. He wasn't like Simon, one of those crazy Zealot types. And he was rich! Think of how he could have invested his wealth in the cause! It didn't make sense.

The disciples couldn't hold it in any longer.

"Jesus, what do you mean?"

"If *he* can't make it, what hope is there for any of us? I mean look at Matthew—he was a traitor to our people."

"What about Simon the Zealot? He hung out with a bunch of fanatics!"

"Seriously though, Jesus, if that guy couldn't do it, what chance do we have?"

Jesus replied, "If you try to enter the kingdom on your terms, in your way, you're right, you don't stand a chance. But if you allow God to do it, then the impossible becomes possible."

By this point, Peter was about to explode. "But we have left everything to follow you! If what you are saying is true, then what's the point? What do we get out of this?"

This was another one of those opportunities for Jesus to lead the disciples to see things differently and to learn and grow. The conversation with the young man was as much a *kairos* moment for the disciples as it was for the young man. He looked like a guy who had it all, who had gotten everything right. They had watched his passion, and they had seen that it couldn't take him all the way. He was still more passionate about his lifestyle. He couldn't give it up. But the experience caused them to ask questions about themselves and the choices they made. It also made them ask Jesus some questions.

Jesus explained the plan for the kind of life his disciples, then and now, would lead. It was a life where disciples would put God first, above friends, family, possessions, everything. It was a life where disciples would be accountable for their priorities in life. It was a life where they would get persecuted for the choices they made, but where they would receive much more than what they had sacrificed. And in the age to come, they would receive eternal life. But in heaven, those who were impressive by the world's standards would not be as important, and those who were often overlooked by the world would be like heroes.

The disciples spent three years with Jesus, learning from him, watching him, discovering what it meant to enter the kingdom of God. Eventually it would become clear whether they would act on the values of discipleship Jesus had outlined.

For one of them it was too much. Judas wanted to live his life by his priorities, not God's. He was the treasurer for the disciples' funds and eventually started taking the money for his own use. He went to the religious leaders to arrange to betray Jesus in return for money. Judas led them straight to Jesus and they arrested him. Later, when he came to the full realization of what he'd done, Judas took his own life.

When Jesus went to the cross, it looked like all the disciples would leave him. Peter had denied that he even knew Jesus, and only John was present at the cross.

But after the resurrection the disciples were ready to move forward (Thomas took some convincing). When Jesus returned to heaven, they gathered to pray with the wider group of disciples. They chose Matthias to replace Judas. On the day of Pentecost they were filled with the Holy Spirit and the church was born.

For the rest of their lives the disciples pointed people to Jesus. They lived as a community, sharing their possessions with one another. They boldly preached the message of Jesus, in spite of the violent opposition they faced. They healed the sick, drove out demons. For most of them, putting God first would cost them their lives. Even though they were nobodies by the standards of their society, they shaped the course of world history. They even had a book of the Bible named after how they and others like them lived by faith—the Acts of the Apostles.

ACTION IS A FAITH ISSUE

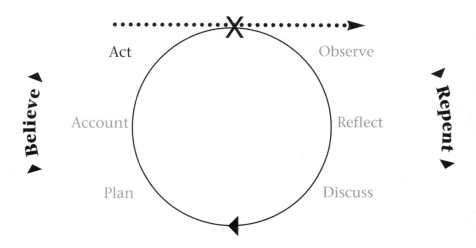

A man's car breaks down on the highway in the middle of the desert in the heat of the day. In the distance he sees a ramshackle old building. He walks toward the building and finds a deserted single room. The only thing inside the room is a table. On the table is a pitcher with a note leaning against it. The pitcher is full of water. The note reads:

> This pitcher contains the *exact* amount of water needed to prime the pump behind this building. If you pour all of the water into the pump, the pump will work.

The man takes the pitcher, goes outside, and looks behind the building. He sees a rusty old pump that looks like it hasn't been used in decades. Will it actually work? The sun is beating down on him and he's hot and sweaty and desperate for a drink. The pitcher of water could quench his thirst. He looks at the deserted highway. If he poured the water into his car radiator, maybe he could get back onto the road and get to a town. But he didn't know how far it was to the next town. He looks at the rusty old pump. Can he risk it?

In the end, the man has to make a choice. He chooses to pour the water into the pump.

The water disappears but primes the pump. It works! He fills the pitcher again and takes a long cool drink. He fills it again and takes it back to his car. He fills the pitcher one last time. He goes inside the building, puts the pitcher of water on the table, and leans the note against it. He returns to his car and he is on his way.

Sometimes, you just have to do something. You throw mud at the wall and you see what sticks. You just have to take the best shot at doing what you can.

You have to make a decision.

Action comes out of confidence. It's a faith issue.

Sometimes our lives are shaped by inactivity, clouded by indecision or procrastination so we don't get anywhere. We return to earlier sections of the Circle. Maybe we reflect a little longer, talk a little more, or make more plans. But there comes a point where our confidence is expressed in how we live. It is visible, it is seen, and it is public. The changes are out there for everyone to see.

Jesus has always been so much more than talk. He preached and taught but he also loved. He healed and lived among people, bringing in God's kingdom. As his disciples, we are not just learning how to think as he thought; we want to live as he lived. A life of faith.

We took the young adults in Sheffield through the Learning Circle in the whole area of relationships. When we reached the Act stage we encouraged them to ask each other out on dates! You could only do the theory of this for so long. The only way to see if it worked was to take action! Go out; get to know each other; see if there is anything in this!

As people started dating, it showed that they were no longer paralyzed by their fears; they were walking in healing and freedom. For some of the young adults it was not too hard; for others it took great courage. They were learning that a life of faith opens the door to new opportunities. In some cases it led to a *kairos* called marriage! For others the next *kairos* was realizing that the relationship would not work out in the long term. But everyone who took a step of action also took a step of growth.

FAITH AGAIN

"I'm back."

Joshua smiled and turned around. He knew the voice of his old friend Caleb.

It had been forty years since they traveled as spies into the Promised Land. They were filled with faith and excitement as they looked at the land God gave them. They were going to have to fight for it, but they didn't care. God had promised them this land. If God could deliver them from a superpower like Egypt, then he could deal with all their other enemies.

But the ten other spies were not convinced. In fact they were so unconvinced that when the team returned to the camp, they gave a report that was so depressing that the Israelites wanted to return to Egypt and go back to being slaves! Things went rapidly downhill after that. The Israelites refused to go into the Promised Land.

The Lord had had enough. He was ready to reject Israel completely, but Moses interceded and God relented. Nonetheless, the Israelites added forty years to their journey in the desert, until the generation that refused to enter the Promised Land had died out. The ten spies who had disagreed with Joshua and Caleb died immediately.

After these forty years, Joshua led the Israelites into the land he and Caleb had spied, the land God had promised them. But Caleb wasn't quite satisfied and traveled to Gilgal to meet with Joshua.

"Moses said to me that the land that I walked on would be an inheritance for me and my children. I believed the Lord had given us this land. And look at me! Forty years have passed, and I am eighty-five years old. I tell you, Joshua, I am as strong today as I was forty years ago when we were spies. And I am just as ready to fight for the land God promised us. So I have one request. Do you remember when we saw the Anakites?"

"The Anakites? You don't forget the Anakites in a hurry. They were huge!"

"Give me the land that God promised me that day. I want to take the giants. If God helps me, I will take them, just as he said."

Joshua blessed Caleb and gave him Hebron as an inheritance. He knew that Caleb had been faithful to God throughout all that had taken place. It was Caleb's time all over again. Only this time, he would receive all that God had promised for Caleb and his children.

The Circle is complete. Once you have been through the Circle, you may find yourself at another *kairos!* It's good to know that every part of our lives presents us with the opportunity to see God's kingdom come. As you put the Learning Circle into practice, you soon discover that life looks like a Slinky, a series of connected loops. Every time you go around the Circle properly you learn something and grow to become a bit more like Jesus—you move one step closer to the kingdom!

Conclusion

*W*hew! What a ride. Now that your brain is crammed full of new information, you may feel challenged by what you've read, and you may even have some great new ideas about how to begin practicing the Circle in your life. But where do you start? I want to encourage you by giving you some points to focus on that will help you come up with a *plan* for putting the Circle into *action*. The first thing you should do is go through the Circle! Maybe reading this book was a *kairos* moment for you. You've discovered new ways of looking at your life, your relationships, or your ministry and now it's time to take those first steps around the Circle as you explore, learn from, and grow through this *kairos* moment.

Start by observing your reactions to the ideas and information presented in this book—write down your observations if that will help you. Then begin to reflect on those observations. Why do you feel the way you feel about the Circle? Why do you agree? Why do you disagree? What parts are making you feel challenged or confused? Now you need to discuss these observations and questions with someone from whom you can gain further insight about your experiences. This may be a little difficult because maybe that person hasn't read about the Circle and won't understand what you are talking about. Why not tell them what you have learned by teaching them about the Circle or allowing them to borrow this book? Both of you will then be equipped to start sharing your various *kairos* moments, discussing each other's observations, and engaging in a meaningful relationship of accountability.

So, your observations are made and you've gotten some valuable insight from someone else regarding your thoughts and questions. Now it's time to come up with a plan. How are you going to do it? Don't be afraid to start small—*LifeShapes* takes practice. Create a plan that allows you to take your idea and make it a reality with simple steps of action. Then tell someone, maybe that same person you had the earlier discussion with, about your plan and your goals so that you are accountable for putting the plan into action. All that's left is to do it! Put your plan into practice and commit to accomplishing the goals you have set for yourself. Now you're ready for some more ideas.

WHY COMMUNITY?

Almost every chapter of this book has dealt with some aspect of community and relationship and how those ideas factor into the Circle. I cannot stress enough the importance of living your life, especially those significant moments of life where God is challenging you to grow, within community. You've read a lot about relationships and community: how clarity leads to community, community leads to confidence, confidence leads to courage, and so on. But let me give you the simple, biblical basis for this principle: Compartmentalization and "individuality" breed isolation, and isolation is the result of our separation from God because of our sins. When Jesus died for our sins and ended our isolation from God, he cleared the path for us to live in relationship with our heavenly Father. We don't want to live a life that says we're isolated from him, yet we do so by ordering our relationships into boxes and separating ourselves from others.

We must choose to live as integrated, not compartmentalized, people. We must choose to live in community rather than isolated on its fringes—this is the way we were designed by God to live. We commit to a lifestyle of community and integration because we are committed to living as human beings. We choose the pain of accountability because we know that pain will produce something useful! I challenge you to adopt this as a lifestyle and there are very easy ways to start working your way into open and honest relationships.

It all goes back to the concept of your community being the setting for you to achieve clarity, confidence, and courage. Begin with your own sense of needing clarity. How do you want to live? What needs to change in your marriage? How can you make things better at your job? You take that need for answers and you seek greater clarity—you need to talk to somebody! As you discuss those questions with someone else, things become clearer and you become more confident about who you are and what you are doing. You have better ideas about how you can change your life. You know exactly what needs to change in your marriage and you have direction and accountability in making that change. You not only know that your job isn't where your gifts and talents are being maximized, but you also have a plan for finding a new job.

Your confidence, brought about within community, gives you the necessary courage and faith to take steps of action. Community is the place where true discipleship, discipleship as Jesus taught us, takes place. So even within the contexts of our community, we not only have a place where we can share and learn, but we can also begin to guide and teach others to do the same.

Remember the discussion about "huddles" in chapter 10? We gave you a list of relational questions you can ask yourself (and others in your community) in order to test the health and balance of the relationships you have in your life. You can also apply the same principles of Up, In, and Out to help you, as leaders within your community, identify the areas of your group God may want to develop. Use these questions as a tool to challenge your group through the process of Repent and Believe so that you can be a part of a healthy and growing community.

UP
- Is the worship in my group dynamic and full of intimacy?
- Do I find it easy to receive guidance for the next step in the life of my group?
- How easy is it to talk to a whole group "from the front"?
- Can I teach effectively from God's Word?
- Does my group share the vision God has given me?
- Do I feel relaxed about leading times of "Holy Spirit" ministry?

IN
- Do members of my group feel cared for?
- Am I effective at resolving conflict?
- Do I take on the discipline of confrontation?
- Is my group living as a community?
- Have I defined my own boundaries well?
- Am I flexible?
- How are my weaknesses as a leader compensated for by others?
- How do I cope with overdependent people?
- How do I cope with controlling group members?

- Are there difficulties in my relationships with coleaders/assistant leaders?

OUT

- Is my group growing?
- Am I too controlling as a leader?
- How welcoming is my group to new people?
- Can all group members identify at least one Person of Peace?
- Am I using leaders in my group effectively?
- Do I find it easy to multiply groups?
- Are those I am discipling turning into effective leaders?
- Is my group effective in regularly doing "out" activity?
- Does my group have a single "people group" in mind?

Learning to practice your Circle skills through discussion and accountability in community isn't the only way to begin seeing how the Circle can change and impact your life. You must answer the call of Jesus and begin teaching others to do the same.

THOSE WHO CAN'T, TEACH

It's not likely you have a complete grasp of the Circle yet, so you certainly can't begin teaching others how to do it! Clear your head of that false notion. If all the disciples felt like they needed to learn more before they could go out and share Jesus' teachings, Christianity would be a dead religion today. Take what you have learned, mix it with a little humility, and start sharing *LifeShapes* with others. Approach your small group or your church leadership and say, "Hey, I don't really know everything about this, I haven't really even been successful at all of it, but this is life-changing stuff. I was hoping we could learn about it together." You will find that as others are impacted by what you have to share, your life will start taking on more and more of the principles you teach about.

Kelly is a firefighter in Phoenix who had a very real experience with the Circle. He was studying the Circle, just like you are, when a *kairos* moment occurred in his life that showed him how powerfully God works when we share with others what we have learned. Here is a letter he wrote to me about his experience:

> Pastor Breen:
>
> As per our conversation, you know that I ultimately want to get to the point where I can teach the whole series on *LifeShapes*. *LifeShapes* has had an impact on my life—in drawing me closer to Christ—but more importantly, giving me tools to use to make "learners."
>
> You know that I am a captain with the Pheonix Fire Department. I have been a firefighter for fourteen years now. For the past two years I have moonlighted and taught a high school fire science class one night per week to approximately twenty high school seniors.
>
> As I have been studying the Learning Circle, it occurred to me that my high school fire science class might be just the place to start my *LifeShapes* teaching career. I would start with the Learning Circle. Teaching this particular class would provide a low-stress environment and familiar audience in which to practice.
>
> The main obstacle I faced in teaching the Learning Circle was how to make it secular and applicable. What could I relate—in firefighting terms—that would take us through the Learning Circle and give my students a depth of understanding that they could later use and apply to their own life?
>
> Here's what I shared with my class: On March 14, 2001, a local firefighter died in a supermarket fire. I should tell you that this guy was a personal

friend and a very excellent role model to my wife and me.

The day he died was certainly a *kairos* event. Time stopped, the curtains between the physical world and the spiritual world were opened, and God allowed us, the fire service organization, an opportunity to learn.

Within three days of the accident, every firefighter in the valley did a walk through of the building. Walking through this building you could see the burned and charred contents that are typically carried in grocery stores. It looked like a war zone. Everything was black and the smell of smoke was strong. The floor was littered with grocery store items and you could look straight up into the daytime sky, as the roof had collapsed during the fire. The reason I relate all of this is because each firefighter had the opportunity to OBSERVE the terrible conditions in which our friend had given his life. How could this have been prevented? If we, as a fire service organization, were going to change our minds about the way we do business (REPENT), then we had to intentionally choose to learn from this tragedy and OBSERVE the conditions in which it took place.

I can still remember driving home from that walk through of the building. There was complete silence in the fire truck. Each firefighter on that truck was lost in his REFLECTIONS about what had happened, why it had happened, what could have been done differently, etc. We wanted to learn from this event and to honor our fallen brother, but we also wanted to ensure that none of us would fall in the same way. This was an opportunity for growth and, in hindsight, we were clearly moving through the Learning Circle, reflecting on events, and seeking to change.

Over the following weeks, firefighters began to open up and DISCUSS with fellow firefighters their thoughts (REFLECTIONS) on what had happened. It would not be uncommon to walk by a pair of firefighters and overhear something about the events of the fire. This DISCUSSION began to manifest itself and soon, the Phoenix Fire Department decided that change was possible (BELIEVE).

A joint Labor Management Committee was created, dubbed the "Recovery Process," by which PLANS could be developed that would lead to growth. Yes, we wanted to prevent a similar incident in the future, but we also wanted to grow as an organization and a culture.

Next, Labor and Management worked together—in relationship (community)—to hold each other ACCOUNTABLE for the plans set forth in the above committee.

Today, we continue to see the fruits of this process in the local fire service. Many of the plans made in the Recovery Committee have been ACTED upon and I feel there has been significant growth in the fire service as a result of this original *kairos* event.

So this is what I presented to my high school fire science class. I was able to take a topic relevant to fire service and teach the Learning Circle. As I spoke every student was quiet. When they are quiet I know that I have their attention. Before I had begun this lesson I had told the class that I had learned about the Learning Circle in church.

Following the lesson one of the students asked me how this "Circle" related to church. I asked the entire class if they really wanted to know. They all said they did. I was then able to take the class through Mark 1:15 and Matthew 6:26 and give them

a biblical example of the Learning Circle. Again, they
all sat in silence and listened.

As class ended, I said they were welcome to stick
around and talk about "church stuff" if they wanted.
A few students left, but most stayed. I spoke briefly
about the upcoming Alpha class and invited them to
join me. I now have my own table of about ten high
school students for Alpha! I am so excited to see
what God does next.

In Christ,

Kelly

From Kelly's story, you can see how teaching others, even
when we're not entirely sure what we're doing, is simply our
response to what Jesus called us to do. And for that, the Lord
allows us to see fruit in our ministry. You too can learn to apply
the Circle by teaching others what you have learned. There are
many resources available to help you present this material. Visit
www.LifeShapes.com to find out more on teaching products such
as leader's guides, workbooks, and DVDs.

WHAT'S NEXT?

I have given you everything you need to start practicing the
Circle in every part of your life. The decision is now yours
whether or not to go for it. I also want to point out the appen-
dices of this book. Appendix A is a well-thought-out
commentary by my friend Dr. Angus Bell dealing with the Circle
and depression. It offers valuable insight on how we can take the
Circle and apply it to past *kairos* events in order to fully discover
the peace and healing God offers us in our life's significant
moments. Appendix B is a wonderful resource for church leaders
who want to discover how they can apply the Circle to the

growth of their church and the health of their congregation or various ministries.

Let me encourage you by saying that practice and failure are truly the ways we become skilled and successful at doing anything. Do not expect to be just like Jesus after your first trip around the Circle. God gives us many opportunities, big and small, every day to work our way around the Circle. Ease yourself into it. Begin to grow and learn from the smaller moments and you will have trained yourself to prepare for the larger ones.

My hope is that as you have read this book, you've seen that the process of the Learning Circle really is the way Jesus taught his disciples two thousand years ago in the Sermon on the Mount and to all who would call themselves his disciples today.

In every *kairos* event you encounter, whether positive or negative, know that it is an opportunity for the kingdom of God to enter your life in a fresh way, for heaven to touch earth.

The process is one of repentance and faith.

Repentance: An inner transformation.

Observe: Look at your *kairos* event with fresh eyes; look deeper; absorb.

Reflect: Ask yourself honest questions about it.

Discuss: Bring your internal reflections to the surface as you invite someone in to share your situation.

And then Faith: The outward result of your transformation.

Plan: Declare your intentions by making a plan for the next step as you move forward from your *kairos* event.

Account: Give someone else the permission to walk with you, hold you accountable for your plans.

Act: Do it.

If that is the way Jesus taught his first disciples, surely it's the way he continues to teach his disciples now, isn't it?

Take the Learning Circle into your workplace, your marriage, your friendships, your family life, your hurts and struggles, hopes and dreams. Jesus will always be the answer to your situation. The Circle is one tool to use as you dig for the presence of God in the landscape of your life. Remember, we are not achievers for Jesus, we are lifelong learners. I am still learning after all these years.

The Circle and Depression

By Dr. Angus Bell, psychiatrist, and Mike Breen

In Bible times, leprosy (a general term used to describe a number of skin diseases, including what is known today as Hansen's disease) was a physical condition surrounded by fear and suspicion. People with leprosy were ostracized from the local community because their condition was deemed incurable.

But the stigma ran much deeper; leprosy made a person ritually unclean and unable to participate fully in religious community life. Later practices permitted lepers to attend the synagogue, but on the condition that they were the first to enter and the last to leave and were in a special compartment isolated from other worshippers.

In a sense, leprosy was considered symbolic of God's displeasure.

In the twenty-first century an invisible debilitating condition is spreading through the Western world like modern-day leprosy. In terms of economic cost it is second only to coronary heart disease, the majority of costs linked to early death and the loss of work. Yet the illness remains something of a mystery because the shameful perception of the illness causes those afflicted to suffer in silence and often not seek out adequate treatment.

This leprosy of the postmodern era is depression. Disturbingly, attitudes from within the church range from suspicion ("It must be sin." "It's a lack of faith." "It's demonic.") to a positivism that verges on denial ("Just pray." "Be filled with the Spirit." "Do a Bible study."). It is little wonder that the overwhelming struggle for most depressed

Christians is keeping the fact that they are taking antidepressants a secret from their Christian friends. The stigma of isolation and shame prevails as it did with leprosy.

What Becomes of the Brokenhearted?

Doesn't everyone long for a passionate life?

We love passionate and enthusiastic people; they carry something of the nature of God with them. In fact, the word "enthusiasm" derives from the Greek word *enthousiasmos*, which comes from *entheos*, meaning "having the god within."

It's as though the human heart was created for passion and enthusiasm, yet as we face life's challenges we can suffer a sequence of losses and disappointments that kill our passion and wound our hearts. Missed opportunities, broken relationships, all the stresses and strains of life that hurt us take their toll. Each event scars our frail flesh; each wound causes a retreat into a hidden place more easily protected.

Eventually we hide our hearts, and our passion is gradually restrained, starved, and weakened. We begin to feel less alive. This is a dangerous position to be in. A hungry heart is a persistent predator looking to devour anything that will give temporary respite to the ache within. Our hearts become more vulnerable to the quick fix, the surge of adrenaline that accompanies impulsive pleasure. Here we discover the territory of addiction: the guilty rush of pornography, the tantalizing danger of the illicit relationship, the "retail therapy" of acquiring even more possessions, borrowing ever-increasing sums of money to finance the next car, house, or vacation. Or perhaps we are drawn to inhabit the darker terrain where the relief of boredom and pain is found in our next fix: a drink, a tablet, a purge, even the comforting pain of self-harm.

Accompanying these behaviors are increasingly unpleasant feelings—anger and irritability, sadness and anxiety, clothed with a fundamental lack of pleasure in life.

When talking about anxiety and depression, most people refer to a "breakdown," and indeed a broken heart is most vulnerable to what we call depression. When severe, depression is a distinct illness with measurable impairment of physical (brain) functioning such as sleep, appetite, sexual libido, concentration, and memory. However, it is also described as "a variable cluster or symptoms," a syndrome that can be expressed very differently in each individual.

The combination of painful emotions and lower sense of worth and ability feels so shameful, especially for the Christian who has to face not only this illness but also the loss of faith that frequently accompanies it.

THE STRESS MODEL: FERRARI VS. FORD PINTO

The best way to explain why a person becomes depressed is by using a stress model. This suggests that a person's susceptibility to any illness is due to an interaction between the physical limits of the body and recent stress, long-term strains, and early life events.

It might help to visualize this model in terms of transport.

Imagine, as you prepared to go to work and approached the garage, that instead of seeing your usual car, you see two! One is a Ferrari, the other an old Ford Pinto. Given the vision that is before you, would you drive each car in the same way? Be honest now! Each car has different fuel requirements, service intervals, and performances. But both could achieve high mileages and carry four adults long distance if appropriately looked after. However, each car handles stress differently and has different stress tolerances described in the manufacturer's manual.

The point is this: We all have been given different "cars" as brains, but the owner's manual is not in our possession so we don't quite know the limits of our design. In ignorance of our own stress limits, we drive ourselves beyond our design parameters. As Christians, of course, we have handed ownership over to the Holy Spirit, who handily is in possession of the original manufacturer's blueprints! The Holy Spirit has been given to us as a guide to successful living and is asking if how are we driving is appropriate for the "car" (our life).

Taking the analogy further, if the heart of the car is the engine, then the heart of the brain is the limbic system. This is placed at the center of the brain like the yolk in an egg.

The purpose of the limbic system is to set the emotional tone of your mind. It has strong links to memory. It also controls motivation or will, appetite for food, drink, sleep, and sex. Biblically, it is your heart! But crucially it is also part of your mind! Feelings and thought are linked both anatomically in your brain and psychologically in your mind. The Bible has been way ahead of us all along; we see in the vocabulary of both the Old and New Testaments that the heart and mind are inextricably linked, referring to a person's thought and emotional life—to the inner person, as it were.

The Bible uses many words for mind/heart: *lev* (thoughts, feelings, will, emotions, desires); *nous* (the mind, the intellectual faculties, a particular mode of thinking and judging, thoughts, feelings, purposes, desire); *kardia* (heart, character, thoughts, appetites, desires); and *dianoia* (the mind as the faculty of understanding feeling).

The Bible has no description of depression as a distinct condition, but it does contain descriptions of unpleasant and emotional states, where biblical characters (heroes) are overwhelmed by feelings of sadness, grief, mourning, shame, bitterness, or guilt. Such feelings are consistently accompanied by lower sense of self-worth and ability.

I am poured out like water,
and all my bones are out of joint.
My heart has turned to wax;
it has melted away within me.

—Psalm 22:14

Why are you downcast, O my soul?
Why so disturbed within me?

—Psalm 42:5

Cursed be the day I was born! May the day my mother
bore me not be blessed!

—Jeremiah 20:14

I loathe my very life; therefore I will give free rein to
my complaint and speak out in the bitterness of my
soul.

—Job 10:1

A *KAIROS* EVENT CALLED PAIN

Leprosy (Hansen's disease) causes cumulative damage to the
body after the leprosy bacterium has killed pain sensation. The con-
sequence of being numb to pain can be devastating. The same can
be true of depression. We are numbed by the pain and indulge in
actions that damage us further: the depressed man who contracts
HIV through casual sex, the bulimic who purges and vomits, the
self-harmer who cuts. All these things may make us feel alive—temporarily. Alternatively, we may simply withdraw from friends,
family, and community.

Often, when we can no longer ignore the warning signs of pain,
the process of change can actually begin.

Most of us have regarded depression as a negative, shameful

experience, using terms such as "breakdown." Instead, it is important to regard it as a possible signpost toward change. Depression in the context of the Learning Circle becomes a learning event, a signpost from God. It may be discipline or it may be guidance, but it is something we need to responsibly process and respond to. It is as though in the valley experiences of our lives, the Shepherd of our souls uses pain as instruments of his mercy and protection, as a rod and a staff in the valley of the shadow of death.

Depression is often a reaction to some form of death of the self; it is intimately related to loss. It is also rarely sudden, though it may be triggered by an event.

Let's remember that depressive illness is often an expression of physical stress in the brain, and you should not feel guilty about seeing a doctor or taking antidepressants. See antidepressants as scaffolding that enables you to get on with repair work safely. Often people feel an incredible sense of shame when a doctor prescribes antidepressants; we feel that we shouldn't need a "crutch." If we are happy to use antibiotics for a chest infection, bandages for wounds, why not antidepressants for depression? If someone was in therapy but came into the office in excruciating pain due to an open wound, we would expect the person's thinking and responses to be affected by the pain, and we would attend to the wound first. The same can be true of antidepressants.

THE PROCESS OF CHANGE: THE CIRCLE AND DEPRESSION

OBSERVE

A man (Mr. P.) who took great pride in his ability as a diesel mechanic became depressed as a result of changes at the workplace. He was put under increasing pressure to finish jobs within a certain time set by his manager, while being told at the same time to meet stringent safety standards. He felt he was failing and became angry, anxious, stressed, and unable to work. There was an acute *kairos* event to which he reacted badly. His "collapse" seemed to be out of proportion to the event, so discussion centered on his vulnerability to the *kairos*. Careful inquiry revealed that there was more! Mr. P. was newly married and felt under special pressure to be the provider because his wife wanted to settle down and have a family.

When he met Angus, Mr. P. was guided through the process of observation. Angus encouraged him to look at his own vulnerability, observe what had caused such distress, and relate the significance of his personal *kairos* (change of work standards) to him, perhaps even using the diagram of the Learning Circle to help him make some observations of this event.

Some find this stage of the process quite straightforward, but others require more time for observation.

Mrs. X. was a lawyer who drove to the edge of a cliff and considered driving over it. She was a successful woman in her midthirties; her husband was a college professor and they had three children. She couldn't understand why she was depressed. Lots of observations of her life took place.

It emerged over time that while in her twenties Mrs. X., a vivacious, adventurous young woman, had a serious accident. She spent a lot of time undergoing rehabilitation, during which time her then boyfriend, considering her now flawed, ended their relationship. Mrs. X. married the next man who came along—an excessively controlling introvert who wanted a trophy wife. Her husband wanted to be her knight in shining armor and often would feed her vulnerability with the things he would say to her.

Both of these cases needed a strong *metanoia*, the process of turning around.

REFLECT

The observation stage leads easily into reflections, where deeper questions are asked. Angus asked Mr. P. various questions: *How did you feel before your work changed? Why do you think it affected you so badly?* On occasions it can be important to compare a person's response to an event with someone else's.

DISCUSS

It became apparent that the real pressure was coming from Mr. P.'s fear of being the sole provider in the family. He was feeling trapped in his role as a diesel mechanic and wanted to look at more adventurous lifestyles. He even had considered immigrating to Canada. It was clear that the vulnerability in the *kairos* was that this young couple had very differing expectations of the future. One was expecting to settle down and be sensible and the other to have an adventure! This stage in the Learning Circle brings a situation out into the open. At this point, the couple did some therapeutic work because the depression had its roots in the relationship as well as the work role.

In many areas of life we value privacy over community. Our therapeutic society leans toward privacy as its primary context and does not access the therapeutic qualities of being part of a community. It could be said that modern man desires independence but fears loneliness. In the emotional and economic cocoon we construct around ourselves we become sick and isolated. The truth is we need community to survive.

It is amazing the degree to which people feel that they are the only one ever to experience the things they go through. Community breaks the stigma and power of shame.

The discussion process breaks down shame, especially in the Christian community where it is already acknowledged that we are broken people with a merciful Savior. Interestingly, shame finds its source of power in pride. People who feel ashamed don't realize they are proud, often with the kind of pride that is invested in one's self-image.

For Mr. P., it became apparent that the value placed on his performance at work combined with his feeling that he was losing a power struggle in his marriage led to a double dose of shame (and anger). The stress of the situation was more than his brain could deal with, so depression developed, and he was unable to function in the situation. Depression becomes a *kairos* event in itself!

At St. Thomas' Church, the power of shame was often broken through the messages spoken from the pulpit, communicated with transparency and in vulnerability. In seeing the vulnerability and transparency of another (particularly in those they respected and admired), people were released to acknowledge and open up about their own weaknesses and problems. It opened the door for people to work things through instead of hiding. After the message, people had the opportunity to respond by talking to someone and receiving prayer.

We can see something of the same idea in the popularity of daytime television with its talk shows. People identify with the people on the screen and connect with their problems and look at their solutions.

In some cases, however, people are so ashamed that they really cannot talk in community and need a few smaller steps to get them into the process of breaking the power of shame. This needs to be done in a noncontrolling way with small groups of two or three people who are accountable to one another. This can be a more effective context. We have to act with caution in these situations; we shouldn't be driving people out into the open; there should be a wooing into openness. The ice melts under the warmth of community.

PLAN

> Therefore, I urge you, brothers, in view of God's mercy,
> to offer your bodies as living sacrifices, holy and pleas-
> ing to God—this is your spiritual act of worship. Do not
> conform any longer to the pattern of this world, but be
> transformed by the renewing of your mind. Then you
> will be able to test and approve what God's will is—his
> good, pleasing and perfect will.
>
> —Romans 12:1–2

It's important to note that without a plan for change, the problems we currently face will return. As we've already mentioned,
medication can be a very important part of the process of change, and
we really do not need to feel ashamed of it.

Making a plan for the future generally means identifying any area
of our lives that has contributed to our current condition. This could
include looking at areas such as:

- Diet

- Exercise

- Relationships. We may need to end certain relationships or
  start new ones. It may be important to take an inventory of
  the relationships we have—are we surrounded by lovers or
  leeches?

- Economic issues. Often people pursue the goal of economic
  success hoping to secure a prosperous retirement, when actually what is needed is downsizing and freeing up time and
  energy for the relationships in their lives.

- Our life's purpose. Sometimes it is important to ask the question, "What makes you feel happy and fulfilled?" Each of us
  has God-given gifts and abilities, but are we using them?
  Mr. P., the diesel mechanic, became depressed after changes
  at work put him under new pressures. He had also recently

gotten married, so he was also making adjustments in his home life. As he unpacked his *kairos,* it emerged that Mr. P. was not only a skilled mechanic, but a gifted artist. He had even been offered a job as an illustrator for a national comic magazine. The concern then became, was Mr. P. living out his purpose?

ACCOUNT

It has been said from various pulpits many times that the problem with living sacrifices is that they have a habit of crawling off the altar. So accountability is very important!

Without accountability, we may not carry out our plan, or we may try to modify it to make it easier or to avoid things we don't want to address.

We need to practice the changes for a number of weeks so that they take root in our lives. If we are married, our spouse needs to be included. Often a key fact of the planning stage is, "Have you talked to your spouse?" Shame has a way of being active in particular relationships, so we often need to ask ourselves the question, "Who else needs to know?"

Accountability groups became a vital part of the lives of the congregation of St. Thomas' Church in Sheffield. Peer groups of two or three people of the same sex would meet together on a regular basis to talk and pray through particular issues and temptations they struggled with.

Another important principle taught and practiced in the community at St. Thomas' Church is the principle found in Matthew 18:15, where Jesus gives instruction on how to resolve conflict productively—starting with addressing directly the person who has offended you.

ACT

We also need a physical, tangible change in behavior. The first three stages in the Circle deal with changing our inner reality; the last three stages address our outer reality. True inner change has to be matched by something that can be observed. The final stage hopefully will lead to a new *kairos*.

YOUR BURDEN, HIS YOKE

> Come to me, all you who are weary and burdened, and I will give you rest. Take my yoke upon you and learn from me, for I am gentle and humble in heart, and you will find rest for your souls. For my yoke is easy and my burden is light.
>
> —Matthew 11:28–30

When we read these words, we often consider the call to take Jesus' yoke as an isolated individual. Actually what Jesus offers here is an invitation to be yoked with him. Being yoked with Christ inevitably means that we will learn how to walk with a different rhythm to the yokes and burdens that have sometimes dragged us through life. This is a situation where lasting changes *to* our lives produce a lasting change *in* our lives. But a major reality we all need to grasp is that these changes and the healing they produce are not found in isolation. For too long people burdened with shame have struggled and suffered alone. But the Savior has offered his body, that we might find rest. And his body—his church—has a vital role to play as an instrument of his healing in the valley experiences so many of us face.

For Church

By Mal Calladine

In the process of reorganizing our church to become a *"LifeShapes* church,"* our challenge as a staff team was to be able to lay the Circle as a template over our big-picture assumptions of what we do as a church. The goal being to see what convictions came from the *kairos* moments that were raised in our discussions and determine how we could act accordingly. How could the Circle concepts challenge us (as a diagnostic tool) in terms of what we need to do more effectively as a church? In what areas are we all about events but no process? As a church, what is our weakest point in the Circle? Below are some of our observations, reflections, and responses as we have patiently allowed the Lord to search our hearts (Ps. 139:23) and use our understanding of the Circle.

We began to see that Sunday was our big event; it was often some type of *kairos* event for most people as the Lord spoke to them in word, worship, Communion, or prayer ministry. But as time moved along, it got to Sunday lunch, sports came on the TV, school and work the next day started to loom large, and all our good intentions would get lost in the shuffle. How could we encourage people to engage in the process of the Circle once they have had the "God event"? How do we help change people's lives and see them aligned toward the kingdom? From our point of view, we were only doing the Repent side, which is really no better than going to the hair salon where you also talk about your events, observations, and reflections but don't necessarily do anything else about it. How could we as the church be more than a hair salon?

PREACHING FOR A RESPONSE

In regard to Sunday morning worship, much of today's church has missed out on the key principle of Isaiah 55:11, which says that the word of the Lord does not return empty but accomplishes what he desires and achieves the purposes for which he sent it. If we just end our Sunday morning service with "see you next week," we have missed an opportunity to see what God's desires and purposes are. The whole idea behind the Circle is *how* we respond to God's teaching. So the question becomes: How, as a church staff, do we "preach for a response"? If God's Spirit is at work on Sunday morning, we need to give people a chance to respond to him. It's not enough to assume that everyone will work it out for themselves once they get home! We are giving no plan for processing, reflection, or accountability—that is the very reason so many people go back to the same way of living Monday morning after Monday morning.

Long ago, I took a seeking friend to a church of great reputation. My heart sank as I realized that this was not a good morning to see the church at its best. The worship leader was clearly brought in hastily from another church, and the speaker that morning (who was very well known) was an effective cure for insomnia. After he finished there was an audible sigh of relief from the entire congregation. As the service concluded, the wise old pastor suddenly stopped. He asked us to wait on God together for a moment. Then he encouraged people who needed prayer or healing to respond just by standing. Many stood up all around. The people who were still sitting were asked to pray for those close to them. The Spirit of God descended upon us and ministered powerfully to all those around me. As we left, my friend remarked that he'd been powerfully impacted by God at that moment. He admitted that the worship and message had been awful and that in any other situation he would have stood up and gone home, home to a life left unchanged. But an opportunity was given by that wise old leader for God's presence to fulfill his word—and that experience blew my friend out of the water. He experienced the reality of God, and it was a moment of clarity he could not deny. He had a memory that would be with him for the rest of his life. He suddenly saw how God could impact his life beyond the walls and experiences of a church service. And he saw that even a bad service could be redeemed by a good response. If we don't give our congregation the chance to respond to God's leading, it simply remains a bad service.

As a staff team, it was easy for us to follow the liturgical formula and expect (in our tradition) that God would fully meet his people in the "consummation" of Communion. This, however, is not the charge of Romans 12, calling us to be continually transformed in the renewal of our minds. We need to realize that we have been in an "altar call" culture where we have assimilated the lie that we as a church only respond to one thing: salvation. This does not fit with the Circle at all. The ongoing process of repentance and belief is our biggest challenge in seeing his kingdom come in our lives. So how do we accomplish that ongoing process in our services? The word of the speaker is often very specific. Whether it is about money, sex, family, work, our past, our future, quiet times, loud times, hard times, or easy times, it always leads to a challenge to respond. Responses vary: commitment, forgiveness, getting right with someone, intercession for others, the filling of God's Spirit, prayer for healing, or just doing meaningful business with the Lord. The message and response may highlight situations and relationships that are not right and require forgiveness or challenge people to commit further to areas that are right, such as seeking God's increased presence, equipping, and anointing. The point is, times to respond provide opportunities for "pit stops" on our kingdom journey—some stops are rest areas of outstanding natural beauty, some are collisions where the police get involved, but they are all memorable events on the journey of transformation.

We've committed as a staff to own this concept and to leave opportunity for response after our sermons. It's normally the speaker's responsibility to have a sense of where and what the response is; if you know what the word is, you should have a feel for an appropriate God-inspired response. Finding the appropriate amount of time and physical space for this at the end of the sermon may be your greatest challenge in implementing these ideas.

The main thing you have to guard against is the possibility of becoming formulaic the other way. Instead of "no response, ever," you could default to "public response, always." Sometimes the best response is to let people take the issue away with them, giving them the time and space they need to work through their *kairos* moment. However, you abdicate the dynamics of the Circle if you don't then encourage everyone in your congregation to have somewhere safe to process through the event, whether it is informally with a spouse, family, or key friends or more structurally through small groups.

FROM BIG CHURCH TO SMALL GROUPS

After a Sunday event, we know we have done all we can to facilitate God's *kairos* moments in people's lives. However, that event is only the start of the journey. In order for that moment to become a lifestyle change, one has to go through a whole other process. And so the next challenge was to restructure the entire church so that we could make it happen.

We knew that the event on Sunday was not where people were

going to process through the *kairos* moments of the worship service. The intimate, committed environment of small groups was clearly the perfect place for this. However, many of our small groups were simply Bible studies where people certainly learned a lot of information but were not necessarily held accountable for applying it to their lives. We felt that processing through life, starting with the *kairos* moment and moving around the Circle, would challenge the small groups to new levels of intimacy. This represents a paradigm shift from traditional ideas of small groups, moving from educational to relational. It is this principle that sets these groups up to be the foundational place where the members of the group could "do life" together.

So how do you make the change? To begin with, the leaders of your church's ministries and small groups must be taught the principles of the Circle so that they understand the process themselves. This has been accomplished most effectively through apprenticeship— one-on-one and small groups of leaders working through the material together. Our church has also tried training evenings with Q&A sessions to try to raise the important issues but this was less effective because it didn't allow for the ongoing application of the Circle, while the continuing apprenticeship relationships did. The leaders who now own the Circle and live it out daily lead very different-looking groups than the ones that don't own the Circle. My favorite group is one that decided that they didn't have *kairos* moments but "*kairotic*" moments, which they would ask each other about when they met. Giving one's own in-house terminology to something is a real sign of ownership! That wonderfully fun bit of innuendo has become a buzzword now for a number of people in the church, and it has helped them to better understand the dynamics of small groups working through the Circle.

Once the majority of your leaders are working with these concepts (and living them out), you may want to introduce the Circle to your church without actually explaining what it is! You don't necessarily have to have a six- or eight-week study on the Circle to start practicing it. You can introduce the concepts and application in your current study or in some other way that doesn't make a "life change" seem as rigid and constructed as a book or Bible study. What we did was to instigate a tradition that through the Lent season (the six weekends running up to Easter)—we would have a "whole church study." Under the headline "Listen—Discuss—Apply," the focus of the six weeks was not on a planned or specific study (because some groups are all about studies while others are allergic to books), but an opportunity for people in small groups to process the same content that was given in the Sunday sermon. This Lent we used *Fully Devoted* by John Ortberg, et al. Each weekend sermon would cover particular subject matter from the book, and the response was a specific call to a change of mind or putting faith into action. We expected this to be the Spirit-anointed *kairos* moment that would impact people. Then, the small groups had a chance during the week to discuss, consider the issues raised, and determine how it would impact their lives. Groups became a meaningful place where the people could hold one another accountable for both the individual and corporate plans they made in response to however God was calling them. They were doing the Circle without even knowing it!

This change led to a change in the attitudes of the people participating in small groups. Suddenly, small groups were no longer defined as a place of study, but as a place to work out the application of study. Most of us in the United States have received much more information than the average pastor in two-thirds of the rest of the world. The challenge is what to do with that information. Do we live lives that are just as effective as those who have "less" knowledge?

Different groups process differently. We provided a study to follow up each sermon should groups decide they wanted something like that. Some groups really used it while others never opened the study guide but discussed where they had been most impacted by the sermon and what changes they felt they needed to make. Some got into smaller groups during the evening to hear each other's plan, to make themselves accountable, and to pray for each other. With this approach we were able to engage a wide range of people's learning styles in the process of the Circle and the result has been a culture that finds it much more difficult to simply ignore the *kairos* of Sunday.

STAFF IMPLICATIONS

Working through the changes of the Circle has also affected our daily activities as a staff. Monday morning staff meetings could very easily disintegrate into, "OK, now that the weekend's over, what's the next pressing thing for us to focus toward on our extremely busy calendar?" If this were the case, we have completely failed to respond to where the Lord was getting our attention over the weekend. The first thing I did to make sure this didn't happen was adapt my Monday morning meetings in the light of the dynamics of the Circle.

My first meeting is with my core team. We exchange feedback about the weekend, have a quick chance to discuss observations and reflections and then we make our general plan for the week. We don't want to be too specific about our plans, because we all know ministry requires flexibility, but we have general targets we can hold one another accountable to as a team. Those targets get written down on the whiteboard in the office.

Our next meeting involves the entire church staff. It is thirty minutes of worship, prayer, and feedback, and everyone in the church is invited. This is meant to be a time of giving thanks, and people can report back what the Lord has done (especially if we have been spread out at different events). This is only about the Repent side of the

Circle—hearing about, reflecting on, and praying about all the Lord has been doing.

Ministry leaders then gather for our main business meeting of the week. This is the more boardroom-type opportunity to reflect, discuss, plan, and account. Our experience has taught us that every ministry of the church should be represented at this meeting by its leader. That leader brings to the table his or her defining issues to which others can then contribute ideas and hold that person accountable. At worst, it's simply information sharing (although just that level of communication is helpful). At best, we are shaping together a response to where the Lord is at work.

If the weekend's *kairos* also led to personal conviction among some on staff, we instigate staff ministry leader huddles (which are covered in chapter 10) about how each person is doing in the light of where God is at work in his or her life and ministry. This allows for a more personal application of what the Lord may be saying. This is *the* most awesome and effective investment we could have made on our staff team, and thankfully they are not just held on a Monday morning!

These are just a few ideas that might help you get started on the Circle in your congregation, in your small groups, and among your church staff. All the ideas are just a different form of "review and plan," built around different groups with different styles—but all of them are informed by the Circle. Together, they respond to the different needs of our church, our staff team, and its smaller constituencies, that the kingdom may come in each. I encourage you to be creative in your application of the Circle, but use the biblical principles behind it to come up with your plan. You will be amazed at how some simple steps of action and faith can transform an entire church community!

The Word at Work Around the World

A vital part of Cook Communications Ministries is our international outreach, Cook Communications Ministries International (CCMI). Your purchase of this book, and of other books and Christian-growth products from Cook, enables CCMI to provide Bibles and Christian literature to people in more than 150 languages in 65 countries.

Cook Communications Ministries is a not-for-profit, self-supporting organization. Revenues from sales of our books, Bible curricula, and other church and home products not only fund our U.S. ministry, but also fund our CCMI ministry around the world. One hundred percent of donations to CCMI go to our international literature programs.

CCMI reaches out internationally in three ways:

· Our premier International Christian Publishing Institute (ICPI) trains leaders from nationally led publishing houses around the world.

· We provide literature for pastors, evangelists, and Christian workers in their national language.

· We reach people at risk—refugees, AIDS victims, street children, and famine victims—with God's Word.

Word Power, God's Power

Faith Kidz, RiverOak, Honor, Life Journey, Victor, NexGen — every time you purchase a book produced by Cook Communications Ministries, you not only meet a vital personal need in your life or in the life of someone you love, but you're also a part of ministering to José in Colombia, Humberto in Chile, Gousa in India, or Lidiane in Brazil. You help make it possible for a pastor in China, a child in Peru, or a mother in West Africa to enjoy a life-changing book. And because you helped, children and adults around the world are learning God's Word and walking in his ways.

Thank you for your partnership in helping to disciple the world. May God bless you with the power of his Word in your life.

For more information about our international ministries, visit www.ccmi.org.